Delta Air Lines

Geoff Jones

PLYMOUTH PRESS

Ian Allan
PUBLISHING

First published 1998

ISBN 0 7110 2605 X (Ian Allan Publishing)
ISBN 1-882663-29-2 (Plymouth Press)

Published by Ian Allan Publishing

an imprint of Ian Allan Publishing Ltd, Terminal House, Station Approach, Shepperton, Surrey TW17 8AS.

Printed in Great Britain by Ian Allan Printing Ltd, Riverdene Business Park, Molesey Road, Hersham, Surrey KT12 4RG.

Code: 9810/B

Contents

Introduction	3
Acknowledgements	4
Delta Air Lines Facts	5
Some Useful Technical Terms and Abbreviations	6
Delta's History: From the Weevil to the World	8
Delta Air Lines' Chief Executive Officer	29
Delta Express	31
Delta Shuttle	38
Affiliated Companies — The Delta Connection	43
Delta's Hubs	54
Delta's Global Partners	63
Delta Maintenance	66
Delta's Operations Control Center (OCC)	70
Delta's Air Museum	72
Delta's Aircraft	74
Delta Air Lines Fleet List	83

Front and back covers: *Boeing 767s in Delta's new livery introduced in 1997.* Delta Air Lines

Below: *Part of Atlanta Worldport's Concourse 'A' which is used exclusively by Delta and claimed as the world's second largest single airline operation. Visible are a Boeing 767-332, Lockheed L-1011-500, Boeing 727-232s and a Boeing 737-247 N378DL (ex-Western Air Lines N255WA).* Geoffrey P. Jones

Introduction

Delta Air Lines is the world's largest airline in terms of scheduled passengers carried: a staggering 103,295,000 in 1997. Its main operations base and hub are at Atlanta, in the southeastern US state of Georgia, now known as Atlanta Worldport. On top of the passenger accolade, Delta's Atlanta Worldport operation ranks as the world's largest single-hub carrier operation. The sheer size of Delta's 560 aircraft operation is almost incomprehensible, with around 63,000 staff helping to fly over a quarter of a million passengers every day on its expanding worldwide services.

Delta has three subsidiary 'Connection' airlines — Atlantic Southeast Airlines, Comair and SkyWest Airlines — and an alliance with a fourth 'Connection' airline, Business Express. It operates its low-cost Delta Express subsidiary from Orlando, Florida; the Delta Shuttle between Boston, New York and Washington and has equity holdings in Proteus Airlines in France and Singapore Airlines. Its growing list of international alliances, together with its own expanding international services, makes Delta Air Lines a world force in the airline industry. An alliance with United Airlines is awaiting US-Government approval and would bring Delta into one of the world's largest airline alliance groupings.

Its roots can be traced back to Macon in Georgia in 1924 and the world's first crop-dusting operation. Delta Air Services was founded in 1928, carrying its first passengers in June 1929; it moved its headquarters from Monroe to Atlanta in 1941 when it was a relatively small DC-2 and DC-3 operator. Delta developed into a major US airline force through a series of mergers and takeovers: the 1953 merger with Chicago & Southern Airlines, the absorption of Northeast Airlines in 1972 and, following the 1978 Airline Deregulation Act, the takeover in 1987 of Western Airlines. Delta then became the third largest

Above: *Ramp activity at Delta's Atlanta Worldport, with newly painted MD-88 N913DL (Fleet No 913) and L-1011 TriStar 500 N763DL (Fleet No 763).*
Geoffrey P. Jones

Above: *On approach to Miami in April 1989, Boeing 767-332 N126DL.*
Geoffrey P. Jones

US carrier measured in terms of revenue.

From the relatively recent days of heavy financial losses in the early 1990s, Delta, helped by management and employees cost-saving measures, an improving US economy and, latterly, by the August 1997 appointment of Leo Mullin as the airline's President and Chief Executive Officer, is now a hugely profitable company. Failure of the proposed merger with Continental Airlines (the US's fifth largest airline) in 1997 has not daunted Delta's aspirations and growth. Always aware of the fierce competition from low-cost fares, other airlines in its home market and the choice its customers have both at home and internationally, Delta has none the less earned itself a major place on the US and world airline stage. This book deals, albeit necessarily briefly, with the airline's 74-year history, its personalities, aircraft, routes, the good times and the occasional bad times. For more information on Delta Air Lines you can access their Web Site at http:/www.delta-air.com.

Acknowledgements

The author would like to thank Delta's staff in London, and in particular Tracey Bowen, Supervisor of Corporate Communications in Atlanta, for their help in the preparation of this book. Thanks are also due to Tony Carre, Barry Wheeler, D. Story and Philip Jarrett for the supply of illustrations.

Below: *The long fuselage of the 142-passenger-capacity MD-88, of which Delta has 120 in service, at Atlanta Worldport in March 1998.*
Geoffrey P. Jones

Delta Air Lines Facts

Founded 1924, Monroe, Louisiana
Headquarters Atlanta, Georgia
President and CEO Leo F. Mullin
1997 Revenue (FY Jul-Jun) $13.59 billion
Employees 65,000+
Daily Delta Flights 2,690+
Delta Destinations 194

Delta Connection Carriers
- ASA (Atlantic Southeast Airlines)
- BEX (Business Express)
- Comair
- SkyWest

Worldwide Partners
- Aer Lingus
- Aeromexico
- Air France (pending)
- ANA (pending)
- Austrian Airlines
- China Southern (pending)
- Finnair
- Korean Air
- Malev
- United Airlines (pending)
- Sabena
- Swissair
- Transbrasil
- TAP Air Portugal

Passengers Enplaned in 1997 103,295,376

Major US Hubs
- Atlanta
- Cincinnati
- Salt Lake City
- Dallas/Fort Worth

Major International Gateways
- Atlanta to Europe and Latin America
- Portland OR, to the Pacific
- New York JFK to Europe and beyond

		In service	*On order*	*On option*
Fleet	B-727	131		
	B-737-200	54		
	B-737-347	13		
	B-737-832		70	60
	B-757-232	91	9	20
	B-767-232	15		
	B-767-332	26		
	B-767-332ER	33	14	10
	B-767-432		21	24
	B-777-200		10	20
	L-1011-1	23		
	L-1011-250	6		
	L-1011-500	16		
	MD-11	14		
	MD-88	120		
	MD-90	16		
Total		**558**	**124**	**134**

(The average age of aircraft in the Delta fleet at January 1998 was 13 years)

Some Useful Technical Terms and Abbreviations

AMT — Aircraft Maintenance Technician. The title is due to replace the current A&P designation for mechanics who work on general aviation aircraft, excluding airliners.

AMT-T — Aviation Maintenance Technician — Transport category. This designation will apply to mechanics entering aviation in the future, the difference from an A&P being that AMT-Ts receive specific avionics training.

A&P Licence — Licences that aircraft mechanics receive upon certification from the FAA. 'A' stands for airframe and 'P' stands for powerplant (engine). Aircraft maintenance professionals receive these licences after completing a technical programme and passing the FAA's oral and written exams.

APU — Auxiliary Power Unit. An aircraft-based unit that provides supplementary electrical and pneumatic power onboard, as well as air-conditioning whilst the aircraft is on the ramp and not under its own motive power.

ASM — Available Seat Miles. Represents the standard measure of operating capacity used by airlines, eg one passenger seat flown one mile.

Avionics — Aviation electronics. Includes communications radio, radar, computers, navigation systems and aircraft systems.

Blades — flat, thin parts that move together and rotate in different parts of the engine, eg compressor blades, turbine blades and fan blades.

Compressor — the first section of the engine, also known as the 'cold section'. The compressor section gathers air inside the engine, and then passes it along to the next section, which is the diffuser section. The diffuser section prepares the air for the burner section, which then passes it to the turbine section and finally the exhaust or jet nozzles.

FAA — Federal Aviation Administration. The Washington-based US Government agency within the

Department of Transportation. Deals with air traffic control, security, field of maintenance, aircraft certification and flight standards.

GSE — Ground Support Equipment. This department maintains vehicles such as aircraft tugs and baggage carts.

JAA — Joint Aviation Authority. The European equivalent of the FAA.

Jet Nozzle — a set of concentric tubes that project from the engine, discharging exhaust.

Layover Check — a maintenance check performed on aircraft remaining overnight in a particular city/airport, before the next leg of the trip rotation. Maintenance personnel check fluids, tyres, brakes and the cabin as well as any items noted as inoperative in the technical log book (tech log).

Line Maintenance — department includes maintenance personnel at all out-stations away from the main maintenance bases. Layover checks and other items that do not require servicing of the aircraft in the hangar.

Material Support — maintains and supplies all parts and materials used by the airline. The majority of the inventory is aircraft parts.

Narrowbody — aircraft with one aisle such as the Boeing 727, 737 and 757, the McDonnell Douglas MD-88 and MD-90.

Stabilizer — a moving part on the aircraft's tail, either horizontal or vertical, that provides stability during flight. Often referred to as elevators or rudder.

Thrust Reverser — mechanism at the rear of the engine, using fan exhaust to decelerate an aircraft upon landing by redirecting the flow of engine exhaust.

Turbofan — gas-turbine jet engine generating thrust through a fan inside a large cowling.

Vanes — blade-like mechanisms that direct airflow through the engine. Whilst vanes look like blades, they do not move.

Widebody — aircraft with two aisles instead of one, such as the Boeing 767 and 777, Lockheed L-1011 and McDonnell Douglas MD-11.

Below: *Taxying out at New York's John F. Kennedy International Airport in October 1987, now developed as a major Delta hub, is Boeing 737-300 N302WA Wally Bird, an ex-Western Airlines aircraft.* Tony Carre

Left: *Pictured in Olympic Year, 1996, at Houston Intercontinental Airport after a flight from Dallas/Fort Worth, MD-88 N908DL bears the special Olympic titling on the forward fusleage, applied to many of Delta's fleet that year.* Geoffrey P. Jones

Delta's History: From the Weevil to the World

Delta Air Lines is so much a part of the commercial air transport scene in the US and, increasingly, worldwide, that its march from a minuscule crop-dusting company to the airline megalith of the late 1990s seems almost impossible. Delta Air Line's roots can be traced back to the southern United States in 1924 when an ominous plague of insects was the scourge of the cotton fields — the boll-weevil. If it hadn't been for this insect, one might question whether there would ever have been a Delta Air Lines!

Moving up from Mexico and into the vast tracts of the cotton fields in the Mississippi Valley, the boll-weevil posed a huge economic threat to the area. At the US Department of Agriculture's Bureau of Entomology laboratory in Tullulah, Louisiana, Dr B. R. Coad was directing research into combating the potential plague, helped by his assistant district agent from the Louisiana State University, C. E. (Collett Everman) Woolman. Woolman was an agricultural engineering graduate of the University of Illinois and an aviation enthusiast who, despite his preference for the exciting times of World War 1 and early 1920s' aviation, kept his feet firmly on the ground for the more certain future of a career in agriculture.

Two ex-US Army Curtiss Jennys were the first aircraft that Coad and Woolman used for the early and rudimentary attempts at crop-dusting. They had developed a promising weapon against the boll-weevil, a lead arsenate dry powder insecticide, but wanted a much quicker and more scientific method of spreading this over the fields than by hand-sprinkling. Congress gave a small grant towards their researches and acquisition of the Jennys but it wasn't until fate took a hand in 1923 that things started

Below: *The Huff-Daland Duster, on permanent loan to Delta from the National Air & Space Museum, was also known as the Petrel 31.* Delta Air Lines

Above: *Delta Air Service's first aircraft in 1929 was a Travel Air Model S-6000B — this aircraft is in fact a 1931 Curtiss-Wright Travel Air 6B Sedan, but preserved in airworthy condition as NC8878 and in Delta's original colours as part of the Delta Air Museum at Atlanta.* Delta Air Lines

to move. George Post, a New York businessman from Huff-Daland Airplanes, Inc, was flying south, when he experienced mechanical problems. He force-landed in Tullulah, discovered Coad and Woolman's experimental dusting operation, considered this to be a commercial opportunity not to be missed and quickly persuaded his company's management back in Ogdensburg, New York, to form a separate division called Huff-Daland Dusters, Inc. Huff-Daland had gained at the time a small reputation for building light bomber aircraft such as the Pegasus and had also developed and built a three-seater, the Petrel.

Operations by Huff-Daland Dusters started at Macon, Georgia, in 1924. There was little experience of aviation there, and a small number of cotton fields, so the first season's operations proved unsuccessful. Coad, still working in Louisiana, kept a close eye on these developments and suggested that the company moved southwest to 'real cotton country', so in 1925 the company was re-established at Monroe, Louisiana.

Huff-Daland Airplanes, Inc meanwhile had moved to more spacious facilities at Bristol, Pennsylvania, and using its reliable Petrel 5 aircraft as the starting point, instigated a 10ft stretch to the fuselage, substituted a 400hp Liberty engine for the 200hp Wright Whirlwind and effectively doubled its gross weight. This was designated the Petrel 31 and it was able to carry 1,500lb (682kg) of the dry powder insecticide. In May 1925 Woolman joined Huff-Daland to take charge of its crop-dusting operations, the techniques now all but perfected, and the fleet of Huff-Daland Dusters grew quickly to become the world's largest fleet of privately-owned aircraft, first with 18 aircraft and then 25. It was a seasonal business though, so during the winter Woolman decided to diversify and set up operations in Peru. It was whilst in Peru that Woolman and his company secured South American airmail rights to fly the 1,500-mile service between Peru and Ecuador, inaugurating the service in 1927 — it was now that he first appreciated the possible value of a passenger service by air.

Back in Monroe, in 1928 several local businessmen wasted no time when the opportunity arose to invest capital by purchasing Huff-Daland's equipment so that Woolman could start his own aviation company. Named after the Mississippi delta which was an integral part of the local

Above: *Over the Dorset coast of England prior to its delivery to Northeast Airlines in September 1958, Vickers V.798D Viscount N6593C (s/n286) was one of 10 Viscounts in the fleet. It was a special model with more powerful Dart 510 engines and greater fuel capacity.* Philip Jarrett Collection

geography, the new company Delta Air Service, Inc was formed in December 1928 with D. Y. Smith, a Louisiana planter, as Company President and Woolman as Vice-President and General Manager. Delta still pays homage to its foundations each year when the airline's annual general meeting convenes in the town.

Delta Air Service's first aircraft were three five-passenger Travel Air 4000s. Woolman then purchased the assets of Fox Flying Services, which included two Travel Air S-6000Bs. On 17 June 1929, with John Howe as pilot, Delta Air Service's first passenger flight took off from Love Field at Dallas, stopped at Shreveport, Louisiana, and Selman Field at Monroe, before arriving safely at Jackson, Mississippi. Additional aircraft joined the fleet and the route was extended west to Fort Worth, Texas, and east to Birmingham, Alabama — a bold move because the service was passenger-only and unsupported by the benefit of a mail carriage contract. On 18 June 1930 Delta extended its route eastwards to Atlanta. The southern transcontinental air mail contract went to a rival airline, American Airways! This competed directly with Delta between Dallas and Atlanta.

Delta and Woolman spent several years retrenching, getting back into dusting. In 1934, now as the Delta Air Corporation, they successfully bid for the revised air mail route (under the 1934 Black-McKellar Act) to fly the new 'Route 24' between Dallas and Charleston, South Carolina, via Monroe, Birmingham and Atlanta. Woolman purchased six Stinson SM-6000Bs (Stinson T) tri-motors from the reconstituted American Airways (now American Airlines) and flew their first air mail service on 4 July 1934 under the name of Delta Air Lines. The airline was subtitled 'The Trans-Southern Route'. This was the stepping stone for the airline's climb to prominence, mixed with the inevitable luck and business acumen.

While Delta was busy in the southern US, three other pioneer airlines that were to contribute to the Delta of the future, were in the same period of gestation. Airline names at the time were evocative of the geographical region they served. Chicago & Southern Air Lines concentrated on the midwest, linking the Great Lakes cities of Detroit and Chicago through Memphis to New Orleans and Houston in the south. Its founder, Carleton Putnam, also founded Pacific Seaboard Air Lines in 1933, flying passengers only from Los Angeles to San Francisco via Santa Barbara, Santa Maria, Paso Robles, Salinas and Monterey. In the northeast US, Boston & Maine Airways served cities in New England, merged with National Airways in 1937 and became Northeast Airlines in November 1940. On the US west coast Western Air Express pioneered the mail-service flights between Los Angeles and Salt Lake City in April 1926, merged with Transcontinental Air Transport in 1930, took over the Montana-based National Park Airways in 1937 and in 1941 changed its name to Western Air Lines.

These three airlines were the main constituents of today's Delta Air Lines: Chicago & Southern Air Lines merged with Delta in 1953, Northeast Airlines merged with Delta in 1972 and Western Air Lines merged with Delta in 1987.

Delta Air Lines itself continually upgraded its aircraft — and its image — during the 1930s. Low-wing, tri-motor Stinson Model As were purchased new in 1935 and Lockheed Model 5C Vegas were used that year to speed the mail flights, Woolman realising that a modern fleet would give him the edge over the competition. A major step forward was Delta's order for five Lockheed Model 10s in 1935, their sumptuous seating for 10 passengers was quite adequate for traffic levels at the time and the type was

Below: *Atlanta airport in 1947 with Delta Air Lines' first Douglas DC-4, NC37472, on the ramp along with an Eastern Air Lines DC-3. Delta operated eight DC-4s, converted C-54s, between 1946 and 1953.* Delta Air Lines

Above: *Delta Air Lines' general offices and hangar at Atlanta Hartsfield in 1947. The hangar, still in existance in 1998, is where the DC-3 Ship 41 is being restored and will hold the nucleus of the new Delta Air Museum.* Delta Air Lines

slightly faster than the larger DC-2s and Boeing 247s being used by the competition. Delta had to go with the pack as traffic increased but it wasn't until February 1940 that the first of four 14-passenger DC-2s purchased from American Airlines entered service — it was an historic moment on 15 March when a third crew member was on board the aircraft, Delta's first stewardess or flight attendant, Miss Laura Wizark. The DC-2s were sold in early 1941, the first five DC-3s being delivered in the space of 36 days in late 1940 and early 1941 (one of these, the second delivered, SHIP 41, is now preserved by Delta — see the chapter 'Delta's Air Museum'). A total of 28 DC-3s served with Delta between December 1940 and April 1963, three of them all-cargo C-47s. In 1941 Delta employed 400 people system-wide and had 10 aircraft: the five DC-3s and five Lockheed 10s.

The year 1941 saw Delta move its general offices and overhaul base from Monroe to Atlanta, which was now central to its north-south and east-west route structure. By 1945 World War 2 was over and the Civil Aeronautics Board (CAB) awarded Delta two important new route licences: from Atlanta south to Miami via Jacksonville, and from Cincinnati north to Chicago. 18 December 1945 was an important date as Delta Air Lines became the official name of the airline, having previously been just an operating name for Delta Air Corporation. It coincided with delivery of the first of seven ex-USAAF Douglas C-54 Skymasters, initially sent to Douglas for civilianisation as DC-4s, then by February 1946 going to Atlanta. Its first DC-4, NC37472, flew the inaugural service between Chicago and Miami on 6 March 1946, followed by the type's introduction on the Atlanta to Dallas route on 1 April. In February 1948 Delta ordered five pressurised Douglas DC-6s, prompted by competition from Eastern Air Lines who were now flying the much faster and more comfortable Lockheed Constellations between Chicago and Miami. The first DC-6 entered service on 1 December 1948, competing successfully with Eastern and causing Woolman to increase his orders for the type to 11, delivered between 1948 and 1958.

On 1 May 1953 the CAB formally transferred the routes of Chicago & Southern to Delta Air Lines as it entered another period of strength and growth. C&S had been operating DC-4s, and Lockheed 649A Constellations, extending its route structure from Detroit and Chicago in the north, through Memphis to New Orleans and Houston in the south, together with international services to Havana, Caracas (Venezuela) and San Juan (Puerto Rico). The Constellations were sold to TWA in 1954 and until September 1955 the merged airline was called Delta-C&S for continuity of identity in the old C&S markets.

With the other big US airlines modernising their fleets and the manufacturers already on the DC-3 replacement bandwagon, Delta decided on the Convair 340, ordering 10 in June 1951 to replace initially its DC-3s and then its DC-4s. Ten more Convair 340s joined the Delta fleet following the order already placed by Chicago & Southern prior to its takeover; eight Convair 440 Metropolitans were added from 1956, and between 1956 and 1958 Delta operated four of its own Lockheed 749 Constellations, bought from PanAm, to provide a service from the south to New York. These were replaced by Douglas DC-7s, 11 of which were ordered by Woolman in his continuing allegiance to Douglas products, and put into service in April 1954 on Delta's long-distance trunk routes, including the important Chicago-Miami. Many other services opened at this time between the northeast and the southern cities of Dallas and New Orleans. In May 1956 Delta switched its New York terminus from Newark to Idlewild (now JFK) as it started to use its full name again, Delta Air Lines. Ten Douglas DC-7Bs were also ordered, the first delivery being in June 1957, Delta promoting both DC-7 variants as 'America's Fastest and Finest Airliner'.

Delta in the late 1950s was still not one of the 'big four' US airlines (United, TWA, American and Eastern) but became the

Below: *Seventeen Convair 880s flew with Delta — N8807E (s/n22-00-29) is seen here. The first Convair 880s entered service with Delta in May 1960 and were initially used on nonstop services from New York Idlewild to Atlanta, Houston and New Orleans in an all-first-class 84-seat layout.*
Barry Wheeler Collection

first airline in the world to introduce the 119-seat Douglas DC-8 jet, on the New York to Atlanta route in September 1959, ahead of arch rival Eastern Air Lines. Delta also broke new ground when the first of 17 Convair 880 jets it ordered commenced service between New York and Atlanta, Houston and New Orleans in May 1960. From seemingly another era, Delta's last DC-3 service, between Atlanta and Knoxville, was flown on 29 October 1960, completing 20 years of continuous passenger service with the type. In 1962 passenger enplanements at Atlanta exceeded 2 million for the first time, 49% of these being on Delta aircraft.

In the years before its merger with Delta, Northeast was also setting an industry lead with its order for 10 British Vickers V.798D Viscount turboprops, and flirted briefly with the possibility of an order for five Bristol Britannia Srs 305s in 1957/8. DC-6Bs soon relegated this possibility to a dream. The Viscounts helped Northeast establish significant market penetration on the New York to Boston route, an early precursor of the Delta Shuttle (see later chapter). Northeast also became the first US carrier to offer a Boeing 707 service on the New York to Miami route prior to its lease of 10 Convair 880 jets between 1960 and 1968. In 1965, the Storer Broadcasting Company of Miami bought a controlling interest in Northeast (from Howard Hughes) and on 10 August 1965 placed a huge $100 million order for 33 new jet and turboprop aircraft. The first Northeast Boeing 727-200 inaugurated the type's scheduled history on 14 December 1967, flying the Miami to New York (JFK) service, now called Northeast 'Yellowbird' because of its aircraft's new yellow and white exteriors. DC-9s (14) and Fairchild-Hiller FH-227Bs (seven) were also part of this order. New routes also opened up to Nassau and Freeport in the Bahamas and on the southern transcontinental route from Miami to Los Angeles. In the late 1960s Northeast's financial problems failed to improve, leading to its search for a merger partner. On 1 August 1972 the merger between Delta and Northeast Airlines

Above: *Delta operated several types as all-cargo aircraft in the 1950s and 1960s. In 1957 five ex-Chinese Nationalist Curtiss C-46s were purchased to complement C-47s on cargo services from Atlanta. N9874F (s/n 22363), Fleet Number 102 is depicted. When the C-46s were retired in 1966, Delta acquired three Lockheed L-100-10 Hercules, which served until 1973.* Barry Wheeler Collection.

became effective.

Out west, Western Air Lines was expanding, with international destinations of Mexico City and Calgary, Canada, being added to its route network in the late 1950s. Under the leadership of Terrell C. Drinkwater, it had expanded with Convair 240s (10 aircraft), Douglas DC-4s (14 aircraft) and a huge fleet of 31 DC-6Bs. In May 1956 it placed an order for 12 Lockheed 188 Electras, at the same time expanding the route network as far as Seattle in the northwest, Edmonton (Canada), Minneapolis in the east and Mexico City in the south — the routes radiating out of Salt Lake City, Denver, Los Angeles and San Francisco. Like all other major US airlines, Western also ordered jets — three Boeing 720Bs in February 1960, soon supplemented in June by two Boeing 707s that had been ordered by Cubana but were undelivered as the 1959 Cuban Revolution cut trade links between the US and Cuba.

Western experienced cut-throat competition on its Los Angeles to San Francisco service from Pacific Southwest Airlines and United, both in terms of aircraft and fares. Western countered this by putting the new Boeing 737-200 into service on the route on 11 June 1968 and its fleet grew to 58 aircraft of various types, some of which were assimilated into the Delta fleet and are still flying with Delta in 1998. Pacific Northern, who merged with Western on 1 July 1967 and had flown aircraft such as the Stinson A, Boeing 247D, DC-3, Douglas A-26 Invader, DC-4 and Lockheed 749A Constellation between 1940 and 1966, entered the jet age itself in March 1962 with the first of three Boeing 720s. Its route network between Seattle and Portland to Alaska and northwest Canadian destinations added a further geographical dimension to Western and subsequently Delta. Western was also a big customer for Boeing's new Boeing 727-247, 47 of the type eventually wearing the big red 'W' colours of the airline between 1969 and Western's merger with Delta on 1 April 1987.

Below: *With Delta's 'Royal Service' logo on the tail of N4880C (s/n 44684), the Douglas DC-7 flew with the airline between 1954 and 1968. The 'Royal Service' was introduced in September 1958, providing a high standard of in-flight catering and ground handling intended to woo the passenger from competing airlines.* Barry Wheeler Collection

Above: *On finals to land at McCarren Field at Las Vegas in April 1982, Western Airlines Boeing 727-247 N2825W joined the Delta fleet following the 1987 merger but has since been retired from service.* Geoffrey P. Jones

In the meantime it had won the right to fly from California (Los Angeles and San Francisco) to Honolulu, starting in July 1969. The first of four McDonnell Douglas DC-10-10s joined Western's fleet in April 1973 and on 9 October 1980 it used the type for a unique Honolulu-Anchorage-London (Gatwick) service, albeit suspended in October 1981. It also inaugurated a Denver-London (Gatwick) service on 25 April 1981 but withdrew from the route in January 1982. Western also formerly established a hub at Salt Lake City, a strategic move as Denver was already dominated by United, and by June 1985 was flying 115 daily departures from this hub. Further feeding into Western's network started in 1986 when it signed an operating agreement with commuter airline, SkyWest (see the chapter 'Affiliated Companies — the Delta Connection').

Delta's own route structure and fleet expanded steadily during the 1970s. At the start of the decade the Atlanta headquarters and main hub had grown to become the US's third largest airport with around 7 million passenger enplanements per annum, of which 46% were with Delta. It ordered the first of a large number of Douglas DC-9 jets — a DC-9-14 (17 joined the fleet) entering service in December 1965 and the first of 63 of the larger DC-9-32s entered service in April 1967. Delta even placed options with Boeing in the mid-1960s for its Supersonic Transport, not wanting to be left behind by the competition. (When the US Senate cancelled the project in March 1971 it did everyone a favour, not least Delta.) In September 1966, C. E. Woolman, the father of Delta, died. The airline he had founded and nurtured was now employing 13,000 system-wide.

Delta's entry into the widebody aircraft market came with its order for 24 Rolls-Royce RB-211-powered Lockheed L-1011 TriStars — popularly known as 'ten-elevens' — in April 1968. This was completely against the run of play and the close ties that Delta had built with Douglas. Notwithstanding, Delta did acquire and fly the rival DC-10, as an insurance, when the 1970-1 problems at Rolls-Royce could have jeopardised the supply of engines, and the TriStars' deliveries themselves. These five

DC-10-10s were leased from United between 1972 and 1975. Other airlines were ordering large numbers of Boeing 747s, but the type was not considered essential for Delta's route structure, so only five (747-132s) were ordered, flying with the airline between September 1970 and April 1977. The first TriStar entered service in December 1973, the type proving both popular and reliable, and Delta ordered more, including TriStar 200s and the long-range, 241-seat, TriStar 500. The most significant route award for many years by the CAB occurred on 21 December 1977, when Delta was awarded rights to fly between Atlanta and London. Inaugurated on 30 April 1978, it was Delta's first transatlantic service, flown initially with TriStar 200s leased from TWA but following the 17 June 1979 start of a second transatlantic service between Atlanta and Frankfurt, with its newly delivered TriStar 500s.

1978 was the year that Congress passed the Airline Deregulation Act. Anticipating this, fare wars between the major US airlines on some of the main trunk routes had already become the norm. On international routes, the granting by the CAB in 1977 of authority for the Laker Skytrain to fly low-cost transatlantic schedules at rock-bottom fares also had its effects. But the 1978 Act, signed by President Carter on 24 October, was to have more sweeping effects on the US air transport industry, including Delta Air Lines, than any other legislation since the early 1930s air-mail award legislation. Delta continued a steady, controlled growth amid the frenzied expansion of some competitors (30 new airlines joined the Regional airline ranks in the first post-deregulation year — People Express, Muse Air and New York Air being three of these). A passenger could now fly coast-to-coast in the US for under $100 and New York-Florida fares could be bought for as little as $55. Delta had to match these fares and, having a deeper pocket than most, was able to survive and to grow. During the dark days of 1981 and

Above: *Douglas DC-8-33 N8038A (s/n 45256) was one of seven bought from PanAm in December 1968 to fly with Delta on services to Europe. They were sold in January 1974. Delta also flew 22 DC-8-51s between 1959 and 1977.*
Barry Wheeler Collection

Above: *First delivered to Delta in November 1969, N1307L was the last of 13 DC-8-61s operated by Delta between 1967 and 1989; in 1982/3 the aircraft were converted to DC-8-71 standard with CFM56-2 engines as seen here in October 1987 at Tampa, Florida.* Tony Carre

1982, when red ink covered the balance sheet because of a severe downturn in traffic, Delta was already committed to an order for the Boeing 767-232, being the launch customer, along with United, for the General Electric CF-6-80 version. Rather than make staff redundant, the airline appealed to its employees for help — they responded by raising $30 million in order to purchase Delta's first B-767, N102DA, which in recognition was named Spirit of Delta, a name it still proudly carries in 1998. Spirit of Delta entered service with Delta in March 1983.

Deregulation casualties nearly included Western. Continental, Air Florida and Wien Alaska all knew this and entered discussions with Western about possible rescue/takeover plans. All these negotiations were intermingled with CAB involvement. Significant savings were achieved at Western in 1983 and it developed its profitable Salt Lake City hub. By early 1984 Western was losing nearly one million dollars a day, but with Gerald Grinstein newly appointed at the helm, it turned itself around to a healthy profit in the first six months of 1985. Delta became another suitor and when in 1985 it offered $860 million for the purchase of Western, it was an offer that couldn't be refused. Western first became a wholly owned subsidiary and then on 1 April 1987 merged fully operationally with Delta, so that Delta Air Lines was now the fourth largest US airline and the fifth largest in the world.

The 1980s saw two of the worst crashes in Delta's long and extremely safe history. On 2 August 1985, whilst landing at Dallas, a L-1011 TriStar crashed during a severe thunderstorm, killing eight of the 11 crew and 128 of the 152 passengers on board. The subsequent investigation identified the cause of the crash as 'wind-shear'. It was as a direct result of this crash that wind-shear warning instrumentation became standard on all Delta aircraft. TCAS in-flight collision avoidance warning equipment is also fitted to all the fleet. On 31 August 1988, also at Dallas, a Boeing 727-200 stalled on take-off — two of the seven crew and 12 of the 101 passengers on board were killed. In all, however, there have been only four fatal incidents involving Delta aircraft since 1970, including two Delta Connection fatal incidents, both involving Embraer EMB-120 Brasilias — one in 1995 (eight killed) and the other in 1997 (29 killed).

By 1982 Atlanta was ranked the world's

Left: *During the mid-1970s Delta operated all three of the currently available widebodied jets: the L-1011 TriStar, Boeing 747 and Douglas DC-10. Delta also inherited Western's DC-10-10s after the 1987 takeover. An ex-Western DC-10-10, N902WA, is seen here at LAX shortly after the takeover, in October 1987.* Tony Carre

busiest hub with over 35 million passengers handled, and by 1987 this figure had increased still further to 47.7 million, of which Delta and its rival, Eastern Air Lines, accounted for 90%. Delta was enplaning 12.32 million passengers at Atlanta in 1987.

Boeing's much-developed 727 replacement was the B-757, which first flew in 1982. Delta became the launch customer for the more powerful P&W PW2037 version in 1980, ordering 60 aircraft. The first of these entered service on 28 November 1984 and by 1990, with 71 of the type, had the largest 757 fleet in the world. Alongside these new medium- and long-range types, the 1980s also saw Delta shopping for a new 150-seat aircraft. Although it got by with Boeing 737-200s for a while, the prospect of the new unducted-fan-powered McDonnell Douglas airliner, the MD-88 (developed from the DC-9-82 or MD-82), was turned into an order for 30 and options for a further 50 in January 1986. First deliveries took place in April 1987, being MD-82s which Delta then converted itself. In November 1989 Delta became the launch customer for the new International Aero Engine V2500-powered McDonnell Douglas MD-90 — 50 aircraft were ordered with options on a further 110. First delivery to Delta was in February 1995.

McDonnell Douglas received another order from Delta in September 1988 for nine of its DC-10 replacement, the MD-11. Delta saw the MD-11 as a TriStar replacement on its intercontinental services to Asia and Europe. Initially two were leased, the first of these being delivered to Atlanta in December 1991 and entering service in February 1992 and these resulted in 11 of the type joining the fleet. The option for 30 MD-11s placed by Delta at the same time was not taken up.

Delta, along with Japan Air Lines, became the launch customer in 1983 for Boeing's new long-range Boeing 767-300. The first entered service with Delta in November 1986.

Delta recorded its largest ever quarterly and annual loss in 1990 (annual net loss of $154 million and operating loss of $227.2 million). This was attributed to the generally weak US economy, low fares from competing airlines such as Eastern and the phenomenal rise in the price of Jet A-1 jet fuel. In July 1990 this was $0.57 per US gal and rose rapidly to $1.40 at its highest — a one cent fuel price increase represented an extra operating cost to Delta of $20 million per annum. Overall during 1990 Delta's aircraft fuel expenses increased by a staggering 53%. Passenger and cargo revenue was increasing but so were losses. Notwithstanding, Delta's management pursued its programme of fleet modernisation and improvements: 36 new aircraft were accepted into the fleet during 1990 and more Boeing 767-300s were ordered. In early 1991 it exercised options for further Boeing 757-200s and MD-88s.

Delta benefited considerably from the demise of Eastern Air Lines at this difficult time. Since its takeover of Northeast, Eastern and Delta had competed vigorously on long-haul routes down the eastern seaboard of the US. Eastern had also been building its operation at Atlanta Hartsfield International airport, Delta's main hub and world headquarters, with 275 daily departures there compared to Delta's 445. A period of intense competition resulted and this, combined with the drastic reduction in passenger figures on all airlines (including Eastern) as a result of the 1991 Gulf War, contributed significantly to its eventual demise. Because Delta was able to take up much of the domestic slack by carrying former Eastern passengers, it felt the effects of the Gulf War less than some other airlines. It had other pay-offs as well, Delta acquiring 10 ex-Eastern TriStars (plus two from Air Canada) and 18 of Eastern's former gates at Atlanta, nine at Washington DC National, three at Los Angeles (LAX) and seven at New York (LaGuardia).

Delta's international growth was slow but sure, Paris being added as a new destination in 1985, Munich and Stuttgart in April 1986, Shannon in 1986, Dublin in 1988, Hamburg in 1989, Amsterdam in 1990, Berlin and Manchester (UK) in 1991, although some of these routes have subsequently been withdrawn. Pacific expansion did not start until March 1987 when Delta inaugurated its Portland (Oregon) to Tokyo service. Seoul (South Korea) and Bangkok (Thailand) followed in December, and Nagoya and Hong Kong were added in February and May 1991 respectively.

Again benefiting from the misfortunes of others, when PanAm went into bankruptcy in 1991, Delta acquired its transatlantic routes and related 'beyond' rights, many take-off and landing slots at strategic airports worldwide, together with some of its fleet, including Airbus A310-200s and A310-300s. It also took over PanAm's Frankfurt (Germany) hub, basing a fleet of Boeing 727s there, and acquired the Boston-New York-Washington shuttle (see separate chapter). The whole asset purchase agreement cost $416 million but it meant that Delta took on 7,800 ex-PanAm staff, honoured $100 million in PanAm passenger tickets and entered into operating leases for the 42 aircraft it inherited. The A310s were disposed of in 1993-5. The last of the DC-9-32s were also phased out of service and Delta's fleet became one of the youngest in the industry with an average aircraft age of 8.8 years. During 1993 Delta added 37 daily departures and five new destinations from Atlanta, making a total of 518 daily departures to 113 destinations and confirming Atlanta as the largest hub operation in the world. Largely due to the acquisition of the PanAm assets and routes, Delta's international capacity grew by 33% during 1993, probably the biggest period of international growth in the airline's history

Left: *A publicist's dream, depicting Delta's Atlanta Concourse 'A' full to overflowing with no fewer than 24 of Delta's fleet visible in this October 1980 photo. At the time, the airline was operating 335 flights daily from Atlanta.* Delta Air Lines

Right: *Western Air Lines opened a Denver to London (Gatwick) service in April 1981 using a leased DC-10-30, N821L named The Londoner. Service was withdrawn on 1 January 1982. N821L is seen here at Gatwick in May 1981.* Geoffrey P. Jones

and matched only by its 1998 push into Latin America. In an innovative move, that in just a few years has set a trend to become a primary airline industry activity, Delta began a service from Atlanta to Brussels in June 1993 under a code-share agreement with Sabena; a similar code-share was also started with Swissair on flights from New York (JFK) to Zurich and Geneva, from Atlanta to Zurich and on a new service from Cincinnati to Zurich. By 1993 Delta Air Lines had assumed the position of the third largest US airline measured by operating revenues and revenue passenger miles flown and was the largest US airline in terms of the total number of passengers enplaned and aircraft departures.

Financial losses, however, were still being recorded ($575.4 million in 1992-3). The Chairman and CEO, Ronald Allen, addressed this problem by a 'challenge' to the airline's employees, 'Leadership 7.5'. Under this programme, Delta intended to reduce its operating costs by approximately $2 billion annually by the end of the June 1997 quarter — it was named Leadership 7.5 because this clearly identified the position that Delta sought in the airline industry and its unit-cost goal. The strategy was to attack costs system-wide so that the company could become profitable in any market, against any competition and at any fare. This inevitably meant a planned reduction in employee numbers, totalling between 12,000 and 15,000. It also intended to become a strong, profitable domestic and international airline poised for growth, and to attain a vision of becoming the 'Worldwide Airline of Choice'. In 1993 Delta identified that more than 50% of its domestic US-origin and -destination traffic was travelling in markets where there was competition from other airlines and as a result average fares were lower and the passenger mile yield declining. By mid-1994 this percentage had increased to 57%, and to 60% by mid-1995.

In 1994 Delta sought to gain access to London (Heathrow) through a code-share agreement with Virgin Atlantic. It was the US Government that dragged its heels on this approval but Delta subsequently succeeded in 1995 when it commenced code-sharing with Virgin between seven US cities and both Heathrow and Gatwick. Delta would still like its own direct access to Heathrow in 1998 and, along with many other carriers, awaits the outcome of the US/UK bilateral agreement.

The economies of European countries in 1994 and 1995 were not as buoyant as expected and this resulted in poor returns for Delta's Frankfurt hub. Overall average fleet age was 9.6 years in 1994, the fleet numbering 550 aircraft, and in an attempt to reduce expenditure, delivery of 37 aircraft scheduled for 1995/6 was deferred so that only eight new aircraft were to be delivered in each of 1995 and 1996. These comprised two Boeing 757-200s, two Boeing 767-300s, a single Boeing

767-300ER and 11 MD-90s.

During 1995 the first five MD-90s entered service with Delta as its fleet total decreased slightly to 543 aircraft (304 of these were owned, 239 leased). Aircraft deliveries up until 2000 were adjusted to total 79 aircraft, 42 of which were MD-90s and 22 Boeing 737-300s. In a major purchase agreement with Federal Express, Delta also agreed to buy between 1995 and 2000 a large number of engine hushkits and spare engines for its Boeing 727-200 fleet to assure compliance with the increasingly stringent aircraft noise restrictions in the US.

By 1995 losses had turned to profits, largely as a result of the Leadership 7.5 programme but also because the US and some European economies were perceived as improving. Rationalisation of Delta's international operations saw an expansion of code-share agreements (Austrian Airlines and Aeromexico) and the start of negotiations for such an agreement with All Nippon Airways in Japan. Services from Cincinnati to Munich, Detroit and Miami to London (Gatwick), New York (JFK) to Stockholm, Hamburg and Lisbon and Dallas/Fort Worth (DFW) to Frankfurt were withdrawn. Services from Frankfurt to Delhi and from Paris to Tel Aviv were also withdrawn, although Delta continued to serve Hamburg through its code-share with Sabena. Transatlantic operations and profits improved dramatically during 1995, mainly as a result of a 10% growth in full-fare passenger traffic and a slight increase in total traffic, even though operating capacity declined by 10%.

1996 was Olympic centennial year, with Atlanta as the host city. Delta was the official airline of the Olympic games and a major sponsor, along with the Atlanta-based Coca Cola Corporation. Delta's MD-11 N812DE was named Centennial Spirit and painted in special Olympic colours to transport the Olympic flame on an historic 7,000-mile flight from Athens to Los Angeles for the start of the US transcontinental torch relay that culminated in the lighting of the Olympic flame in Atlanta and the opening of the games. Spirit of Delta, the employee-purchased Boeing 767-200, was also painted in similar special Olympic colours. 1996 also saw the culmination of protracted negotiations with Delta pilots — this enabled their new Orlando-based, low-cost, Delta Express operation to begin (see later chapter) in Orlando on 1 October.

In 1996 Delta announced that it was to start retiring its L-1011s and in particular

Below: *Delta Lockheed L-1011-500 TriStar N752DA taxying for take-off at Orlando in April 1984.* Geoffrey P. Jones

to replace L-1011s on its transatlantic services with MD-11s and Boeing 767-300s. The plan was to permanently retire some of its older L-1011-1s and 200s used on its domestic US schedules and to substitute reconfigured L-1011-500s. The company ordered 12 additional 767-300ERs but cancelled its large order with Boeing for 52 737-300s and the 56 options. However, it reached agreement with the Nordam Group, Inc to purchase 25 shipsets of Stage 3 engine hushkits for some of its Boeing 737-200 fleet and also placed options for a further 30 shipsets. The fleet size at mid-year in 1996 was 539 aircraft.

Operating revenues increased in 1996 and were split 75% from domestic passengers, 18% from international passengers, 4% from cargo and 3% from other sources. The overall operating income (surplus of income over expenditure) was a record $1,300 million, the company's best ever, although with other costs the net income was $662 million, another record and a 125% improvement over 1995. The Leadership 7.5 programme was working but the company was, and remains, acutely aware of the threat to operating results from the competition from low fares both in its domestic and international markets. In retrospect, Delta has reported profitable annual trading in almost every year since 1947, with the exception of 1983 and the years 1991 to 1994 inclusive.

The rise and rise of the US airline industry in the late 1990s was no better illustrated than by Delta's 1997 results with its operating income rising still further over 1996's figure, to $1,600 million and its net income to $886 million. It also saw a turnaround in the number of cities and countries served by Delta as an expansion started (see table), buoyed by the excellent financial results.

Delta's 1990s Turnaround

Year (ending 30/6)	*Cities served*	*Countries served*	*Operating employees*	*Loss/income (millions $)*
1992	219	34	77,907	-674.9
1993	216	33	73,533	-575.4
1994	210	32	69,000	-447.0
1995	204	31	59,717	+661.0
1996	178	25	60,250	+1,300.0
1997	190	38	62,450	+1,600.0

Right: *A pair of newly delivered Boeing 757-232s sit outside the TOC at Atlanta in April 1991 — a TriStar is seen departing in the distance.*
Geoffrey P. Jones

1997 was also a landmark year at Delta with Ronald W. Allen's retirement as Chairman, President and CEO after 34 years of service. His place was taken by Leo Mullin (see separate chapter). It was also the year that Delta reached an understanding with Boeing for a 10-year agreement on exclusivity for aircraft orders — this was subsequently extended and signed by Delta and Boeing as a 20-year deal for 644 aircraft, giving sole-supplier rights, although the rights of Boeing to sign such exclusivity provisions have been questioned by the European Commission (EC). The deal supports the replacement and rationalisation of Delta's domestic fleet, covering 106 firm aircraft orders from 1998 through to 2006 and valued at $6.7 billion. In addition, there are options on a further 124 aircraft and 'rolling options' on another 414 for delivery through to the year 2018. Engine choices for these aircraft have yet to be made. In April 1997 Delta also placed options on orders for 10 Rolls-Royce Trent 800-powered Boeing 777-200s for delivery in 1999 — these options for 777s were firmed up in November 1997 in a deal worth approximately $1.42 billion. A further 20 Boeing 777s have been placed on option, with 'rolling options' on a further 30. Doubt was cast at the time of the agreement with Boeing on the 16 options Delta held for MD-11s, albeit the takeover of McDonnell Douglas by Boeing has since been ratified. Delta's 60 options for Boeing MD-90s are expected to stay in place. The long-term objective is for Delta to reduce its aircraft family types from six to three whilst replacing older aircraft types with newer Boeing 767s and 737s. L-1011s and Boeing 727s are the two types earmarked for retirement, 767s replacing the L-1011s and 737s the 727s.

The prospect of Boeing 777s arriving with Delta earlier than the originally planned August 1999 deliveries has come and gone. With the 1998 economic crisis in the Far East, Malaysian flag carrier Malaysia Airlines (MAS) was in discussion with Delta over a possible 'off-loading' of up to five Trent 800 Boeing 777s it was scheduled to receive in 1998. Difficulties with crew and staff training for an earlier than scheduled 777 introduction, together with variations in price paid by the two airlines, are the two primary reasons why Delta did not proceed with this plan.

Right: *Britain's first glimpse of the new Boeing 767 was at the September 1982 Farnborough Air Show when N102DA in Delta Air Lines colours was one of the show-stoppers along with the new Boeing 757.*
Geoffrey P. Jones

1997 saw the Frankfurt hub closed and the aircraft redeployed back to the US. However, other international routes were strengthened and added. By 15 August 1997 total transatlantic services from Delta's three hubs at New York (JFK), Atlanta and Cincinnati had expanded to 245 weekly flights to 26 European cities. Delta now had a bigger percentage share in the North Atlantic market (in terms of revenue passenger miles) than any other US airline (19%, with American and United both at 18%) — this statistic was complemented

Right: *As a result of Delta's acquisition of some of PanAmerican's assets in 1991, it operated some ex-PanAm Airbus 310-200s and 300s, including N805PA seen here at Atlanta in 1992. This aircraft was sold to small-package carrier Federal Express in 1994, becoming N420FE.* Delta Air Lines

by a similar top position in the North American domestic market (26%, with American and United at 22% and 18% respectively).

After 35 years, 1997 saw Delta introduce the first major change to its livery on 10 April. Retaining the core colours of red, white and blue, the new livery was claimed to be a bold contemporary look, designed for Delta by Landor Associates of London who have created new identities for over 30 of the world's top airlines including British Airways, Singapore Airlines and Northwest Airlines. The objective of the new colours was not to be too radically different, Delta wanting to update its image but at the same time not alienate its tens of thousands of loyal customers who had grown to know and recognise the traditional Delta look. The new livery will be applied to all 550+ aircraft in Delta's fleet as the aircraft are scheduled for their normal repainting over the next three years (with the obvious exception of new aircraft). This will keep Delta's Atlanta specialist three-bay paint-spray facility (see separate chapter on Maintenance) extremely busy.

Delta's Atlantic Excellence alliance with partners Swissair, Austrian Airlines and Sabena received anti-trust immunity from the US Department of Transportation at the end of 1996. This allowed the four airlines to provide seamless services to customers worldwide by the synchronisation of flight schedules, joint marketing programmes, co-ordinated pricing and integrated frequent flyer programmes. 1997 saw Delta start services from both Atlanta and Cincinnati to São Paulo and Rio de Janeiro in Brazil, and conclude an alliance agreement with Transbrasil. A code-share with Aeromexico was also signed for Delta services from Los Angeles, Dallas/Fort Worth and Atlanta to several Mexican destinations. These first steps towards a Latin American presence by Delta quickly changed to a flood in December 1997 when it announced a major extension of services into Central and South America in a bid to expand its Atlanta hub into a major Latin American gateway. It also marked the change of name for Atlanta Hartsfield International Airport to 'Atlanta Worldport'. The philosophy behind this was explained by Delta's Vice President of Marketing Development, Mark Drusch: 'Airlines are designed to start new things! Delta's Latin American expansion in 1998 results from our more recent success in new services to Brazil and Mexico along with our longer-term overall success in international markets. There are three other main reasons:

- Atlanta Worldport is ripe for development because only 25% of Delta's passengers here are local, the rest coming to Atlanta from the rest of the US and the world.
- The Latin American market is forecast to have a higher growth rate in the next 10 years than even the Pacific/Asian

market. In the last eight years revenue per aircraft seat mile (ASM) into Latin America has grown faster than revenue elsewhere, underlining how vibrant this market is.

- Geographically, South America is directly south of most of the Eastern US where Delta is dominant. Atlanta Worldport is better situated than even Miami, particularly as far as connecting flights are concerned.'

On 5 April 1998 nonstop services by Delta started between Atlanta Worldport and Costa Rica, El Salvador, Guatemala and Panama. Other new services followed during 1998 to Argentina, Belize, Bolivia, Colombia, Ecuador, Paraguay and Uruguay. Delta was also expected to start new services to both Peru and Chile (see separate chapter on Alliances). Services from New York (JFK) to Latin America have also been increased, including São Paulo. Further 1998 international expansion sees the relaunch of the Atlanta Worldport-Hamburg service and New York (JFK) to Stockholm, both in May, although combined at the same time with cessation of the service to Berlin and Copenhagen. A new New York (JFK) to Warsaw service started in March and a Barcelona service started in summer 1998.

In another radical new international move, Delta has started a direct Atlanta Worldport to Tokyo service in 1998 using modified MD-11s with additional fuel capacity, a standard McDonnell Douglas modification. Direct services to Osaka and Fukuoka from Portland (Oregon) have also commenced, Delta perceiving its Japanese market to be mainly business travellers rather than the more volatile tourist traffic that has seen declining fortunes for some transpacific and intra-Asia airlines.

1997's success at Delta was confirmed on 22 December when Margaret Mack made aviation history, boarding Delta flight No 680 from Dallas/Fort Worth to Atlanta Worldport to become the airline's 100 millionth customer in 1997, a feat never before achieved by any airline in one year. It also confirmed Delta as the top airline in the world by scheduled passengers carried — the final figure for 1997 was 103,295,376 passengers enplaned. The statistics change almost daily, but Delta Air Lines, Delta Express, the Delta Shuttle, the Delta Connection carriers and Delta's worldwide partners now operate more than 4,910 flights each day to over 324 cities in 45 countries.

In a hugely significant move that has seen the US major airlines 'grouping' following the signing in January 1998 of an alliance between Northwest Airlines and Continental Airlines, Delta has proposed an alliance or 'pact' with United Airlines. This now may not take place as it is still subject to US Government approval.

Left: *Delta Air Lines Frankfurt Main hub, operated by Delta following the failure of PanAmerican in 1991 until its closure in 1997, although Delta still operate to and from Frankfurt. At one time in 1993, Delta had eight Boeing 727s based at Frankfurt and was operating nonstop flights to 18 destinations from here in Europe, Asia and North America.* Geoffrey P. Jones

Delta Air Lines Latin America Service

Current Service

Country	*City*	*Origination point(s)*	*Delta connection carrier*	*Aircraft*
Brazil	São Paulo	Atlanta	Delta	B-767
		Cincinnati	Delta	B-767
		Miami	Transbrasil	B-767
		New York	Transbrasil	B-767
		Orlando	Transbrasil	B-767
		Washington DC	Transbrasil	B-767
	Brasilia	Miami	Transbrasil	B-767
		New York	Transbrasil	B-767
		Orlando	Transbrasil	B-767
		Washington DC	Transbrasil	B-767
	Rio de Janeiro	Atlanta	Delta	B-767
		Cincinnati	Delta	B-767
		Miami	Transbrasil	B-767
		New York	Transbrasil	B-767
		Orlando	Transbrasil	B-767
		Washington DC	Transbrasil	B-767
Mexico	Cancún	Atlanta	Aeromexico	MD-80
	Guadalajara	Los Angeles	Delta	B-727
			Aeromexico	MD-80
	Leon	Los Angeles	Aeromexico	MD-80
	Mérida	Miami	Aeromexico	MD-80
	Mexico City	Atlanta	Delta	B-757
		Dallas/Ft Worth	Aeromexico	DC-9
		Houston	Aeromexico	DC-9
		Los Angeles	Delta	B-757
		New York	Delta	B-757
		Orlando	Aeromexico	MD-80
	Puerto Vallarta	Los Angeles	Aeromexico	MD-80

Phase One Expansion

Country	*City*	*Filling date*	*Estimated start of service*	*Origination point(s)*	*Aircraft*
Argentina	Buenos Aires	10.12.97	tba	Atlanta New York	B-767-300ER
Brazil	São Paulo	21.11.97	01.10.98	New York	B-767-300ER
Chile	Santiago	22.04.97	tba	Atlanta	B-767-300ER
Colombia	Bogota	10.12.97	tba	Atlanta	B-757
Costa Rica	San José	10.12.97	04.04.98	Atlanta	B-757
El Salvador	San Salvador	10.12.97	04.04.98	Atlanta	B-757
Guatemala	Guatemala City	10.12.97	04.04.98	Atlanta	B-757
Panama	Panama City	10.12.97	04.04.98	Atlanta	B-757
Peru	Lima	13.11.97	04.04.98	Atlanta	B-757
Uruguay	Montevideo	10.12.97	tba	New York	B-767-300ER
Venezuela	Caracas	12.06.97	01.02.98	Atlanta	B-757

Phase Two Expansion

Country	*City*	*Filling date*	*Estimated start of service*	*Origination point(s)*	*Aircraft*
Belize	Belize City	tba	tba	Atlanta	tba
Brazil	Rio de Janeiro	tba	tba	Atlanta	tba
				New York	tba
Bolivia	La Paz	tba	tba	New York	tba
Chile	Santiago	tba	tba	New York	tba
Colombia	Bogota	tba	tba	New York	tba
Ecuador	Guayaquil	tba	tba	Atlanta	tba
	Quito	tba	tba	New York	tba
Honduras	Tegucigalpa	tba	tba	Atlanta	tba
	San Pedro Sula	tba	tba	Atlanta	tba
Nicaragua	Managua	tba	tba	Atlanta	tba
Paraguay	Asunción	tba	tba	New York	tba
Peru	Lima	tba	tba	New York	tba
Venezuela	Caracas	tba	tba	New York	tba

Note: All New York flights originate from JFK International Airport.
All Washington DC flights originate from Dulles International Airport.

Left: *Nosed in at the gate at Minneapolis/St Paul in June 1995, Boeing 727-232 N494DA wears the titling The Official Airline 1996 Olympic Games on the forward fuselage.* Geoffrey P. Jones

Left: *Around 5,000 Delta employees work the ramp areas at Atlanta Worldport. Baggage handling is one of the most important duties in helping rapid turn-arounds and speedy transfers through the world's busiest hub operation. Here a Boeing 757 is unloaded.* Geoffrey P. Jones

Delta Air Lines' Chief Executive Officer

Effective from 31 July 1997, Ronald W. Allen retired as Chairman of the Board, President and Chief Executive Officer (CEO) of Delta Air Lines, Inc. Allen had been with Delta for 34 years. In a boardroom shake-up, Allen, the airline's long-time Chairman and Chief Executive who had joined the airline in 1963 was ousted, allegedly as a result of a power struggle headed by another board member, Gerald Grinstein. Grinstein is quoted as saying, 'We needed to take a fresh look at the way things are done.'

Allen's replacement, Leo F. Mullin, was appointed on 15 August 1997 in a surprise move, as Mullin came to the airline industry from outside the USA's third largest carrier, breaking with the Delta tradition of promoting from within its own management organisation. With Mullin, Grinstein was named Non-Executive Board Chairman, although he does not handle the airline's day-to-day business. A Delta Air Lines 'veteran', Maurice Worth, was appointed to replace Allen as Delta's Chief on an acting basis between Allen's departure and Mullin's arrival, also being promoted to Chief Operating Officer in charge of routine airline operations.

The 54-year-old Mullin is a Harvard College and Harvard Business School graduate, receiving a degree in engineering and applied physics, a degree in applied mathematics and an MBA. He worked for Conrail in Philadelphia, then in a senior position at the First Chicago Bank (the US's 10th largest commercial bank) for 15 years, and he served as Chairman and CEO of the American National Bank in the early 1990s. More recently he served as vice-chairman of Unicom and its chief subsidiary, Commonwealth Edison, the Chicago-area utilities company. He is also a member of the board of the Air Transportation Association of America.

In announcing Mullin's appointment Grinstein said that he was chosen because of his past strategic planning expertise in highly competitive consumer businesses. His lack of airline experience was ignored, but together with Maurice Worth's appointment, Delta had the confidence to look outside the airline industry for their new CEO.

In the months since his appointment, Delta's staff appear to have warmed to Mullin. Writing in Delta Air Lines' 1997 Annual Report, Mullin says, '...(our) focus on customer service and on operational efficiency means our shareholders should expect superior financial returns. It is a function of any business organisation to produce value that yields these superior returns for shareholders. All of us at Delta will remain highly cognizant of that goal as we move forward. The critical task is to increase positive momentum and build a winning organisation — superior in all the respects to which we aspire. Thank you for your support in this early, invigorating period of my association with Delta.'

Previous Delta (and Associated Companies) 'Chiefs'

Harold R. Harris	— 1924 Huff-Daland Dusters Operations Manager
Alfred Frank	— 1927 founder of National Parks Airways
Collett Everman (C. E.) Woolman (Vice-President and General Manager)	— 1928 Delta Air Service
Harris M. (Pop) Hanshue	— 1925 founder and President of Western Air Express
Harris Hanshue	— 1930 President of Transcontinental and Western Air (TWA)
Carleton Putnam	— 1933 founder of Pacific Seaboard Airlines
Clarence E. Faulk	— 1935 President Delta Air Lines
Alvin P. Adams	— 1934 President of Western Air Express Corporation
Paul Collins	— 1933 founded National Airways, Inc. (Central Vermont Airways/ Boston — Maine Airways) and subsequently Northeast Airlines
George Gardner	— 1947 President of Northeast Airlines
Terrell C. Drinkwater	— 1947-90 President of Western Air Lines

Catherine Fitzgerald	— first female executive of Delta
George B. Storer	— 1965-72 gained a controlling interest in Northeast Airlines until its merger with Delta
C. H. 'Charlie' Dolson	— 1965-71 first as President of Delta and then from 1970 as Chairman
J. Judson Taylor	— 1968-71 President of Western Air Lines
Arthur Kelly	— 1972-5 President of Western Air Lines
W. T. 'Tom' Beebe	— 1970-1 President of Delta then Chairman from 1970-80
David Garrett	— 1971-83 President of Delta and also Chairman from 1980-3
Gerald Grinstein	— 1984-6 Chairman of Western Air Lines until its merger with Delta
Ronald W. Allen	— joined Delta in 1963, became President and CEO on November 1983, Chairman and CEO in August 1987 and Chairman, President and CEO in August 1990.

Above; *Leo F. Mullin, appointed Delta Air Lines President and Chief Executive Officer in August 1997.* Delta Air Lines

Right: *With a backdrop of the downtown Atlanta skyline, Boeing 757-232 N664DN takes off from Atlanta Worldport's runway 27R as another 757 awaits clearance to cross the main runway and proceed to the ramp area.* Geoffrey P. Jones

Delta Express

Established in 1996 and flying its first service on 1 October 1996, Delta Express is Delta Air Lines' voyage into the world of low-cost carriers. Most of the 'majors' have established low-cost carriers in the last decade with varying degrees of success but the perceived success of Southwest Airlines is the stimulus to these US airlines to emulate them. Continental Lite came and went, Shuttle by United developed on the US West Coast and USAirways has established its Metrojet operation based at Washington/Baltimore. Casting a glance over its shoulder to Europe, Delta was also conscious of the growth of similar carriers in the UK such as easyJet and Debonair.

In 1994 Delta's then Chairman, Ron Allen, put out a call to Delta's personnel worldwide to take their leading position in the airline industry in order to reduce costs, create new opportunities and meet competition everywhere head-on. At that time Delta said, 'It's likely that the restructuring will result in a higher frequency, low-cost operation in certain short-haul markets as costs are reduced.'

In April 1996 a small team of Delta employees headed by W. E. 'Skip' Barnette and Paulette Corbin sat down to look at low-cost operations. They looked closely at those things that had worked for these other carriers and those that had not, they tried to understand the mechanics of all the various aspects of such an operation and to create a successful product. It was part of a major 'front-line' initiative at Delta for all staff to look at the airline's products.

The Florida leisure market was identified as the market ripe for attack by Delta. The airline was already quite strong in Orlando and its commuter partner, Comair, was based there. The objective was to affect these operations as little as possible but to stimulate new business by attracting those travellers who may otherwise have driven, or come by coach or train. Markets were looked at first and the 50 top markets into Orlando were identified, the cities then

Below: *Landing at Washington (Dulles) International airport in June 1990, Delta Air Lines Boeing 737-247 N375DL (s/n 23602) is Fleet No 375, ex-N248WA of Western Air Lines. The aircraft is now one of the Delta Express fleet based in Orlando, Florida.* Geoffrey P. Jones

Above: *Casual uniforms worn by Delta Express cabin crews.* Delta Air Lines

being slowly eliminated one-by-one. In June 1996 Delta started to test operational and customer service procedures on certain of its existing 'main-line' weekend flights to and from Orlando. These included time-and-motion studies on passengers leaving the aircraft, servicing of the aircraft, the boarding process and push-back from the jetway.

It had already been established that the best aircraft to use on such services would be the Boeing 737-200 of which Delta had 54 in its fleet. In August 1995 the pilot contracts had been agreed and signed for several years hence, making it possible for the 737-200 crews to operate these new services. If 737-200s were to be used, this limited the market due to the aircraft's range, so that flights from Los Angeles, for example, were immediately dismissed. Delta's team also backed away from its big hubs at Atlanta, Cincinnati, Dallas/Fort Worth and Salt Lake City, as services from these locations would not keep the aircraft in the air for long enough. All these processes and factors were pulled together, along with the actual studies at Orlando, to enable Delta to establish what its new product would look like. At 19min, fuelling the aircraft at turnaround was identified as the longest single operation, so this was the main figure around which all the other factors were pitched. Times for cleaning of the aircraft, previously done entirely on the ground, could be reduced if the process was started in the air by the flight attendants, assisted by the passengers. Restocking the aircraft could be accelerated and a modular system was devised for cans of drinks — the only in-flight refreshment — to be served, a predetermined number of drinks being established for two return flights and the specially designed module loaded quickly.

August 1996 saw the team announce Delta Express as a low-fare initiative, operated as a business unit within Delta Air Lines. Its new market centred on Orlando and served four other Florida cities and 10 northeastern and midwest cities.

Delta Air Lines' total involvement in Delta Express was always primary. There was no hiding the fact that the 119-seat configured 737-200s were Delta aircraft, maintained by Delta to its rigorous standards. Their average 737-200 fleet age at the time was 12.2 years, and they were flown by Delta pilots with Delta in-flight personnel serving the customers. It was clearly a Delta product although as a concession, new more casual uniforms were designed for the flight attendants, partly to emphasise the leisure market that they were targeting. Delta Express launched its first service on 1 October 1996, only five months after the initial meeting tasked with investigating the possibility of this new product. Immediately, Delta Express launched into its scheduled services involving 62 daily flights and in-flight aircraft utilisation of around 12hr/day. Delta Express was profitable from 'day one', albeit it did not have to buy new aircraft, pay separate insurance, etc. However, Delta Express's costs are fully allocated, an accounting charge being made for aircraft costs, maintenance, personnel, etc and all other items.

Fare levels were established after a study of the market-place and pitched accordingly. In market research Delta customers had stated that one of the

Above: *Delta's new colours represented on McDonnell Douglas MD-11 N802DE and Boeing 767-332 N193DN.* Delta Air Lines

Above: *A busy ramp scene at Atlanta Worldport during a morning 'bank', with the tails of Delta Boeing 727s, Boeing 757s and McDonnell Douglas MD-88s.* Geoffrey P. Jones

biggest nightmares was the complexity of the fares. Delta Express immediately established a three-tier system: walk-up fares, a seven-day fare and a 21-day fare. It only sells one-way fares and has established a special toll-free 1-800 telephone line for direct booking, used by both the public and travel agents. Seat reservations are offered — an option the other low-cost carriers do not give, Delta Express does not give advanced boarding cards because it wants to avoid high 'no-show' figures and it also offered mileage credits on Delta's mainline frequent flyer programme (SkyMiles). Delta Express fares are also published on the Internet in real time.

All reservations staff for Delta Express are based in Boston, whilst all flight attendants and pilots are based in Orlando, this latter station now accommodating over 2,000 staff and including 300+ pilots. By 1 January 1997, further destinations were added and the number of daily Delta Express flights were up to 128. There was deliberately no overlap with the Delta mainline services, and in fact Delta Express enhanced capacity and revenue on some of the established mainline services by freeing up seats. Now that Delta Express was flying direct from Boston to Orlando, for example, leisure travellers who had previously used Delta on this route travelled Boston-Atlanta and then Atlanta-Orlando, so both these mainline Delta services benefited from Delta Express's existence.

The Boeing 737-200 proved to be an excellent choice, a further aircraft being added in January 1998. There is the facility to increase the fleet using the whole of Delta's 54 737-200s if necessary and if replacement aircraft are available and delivered. Delta Express is continually looking at other markets from its original list of 50 cities. Three new destinations out of Orlando were added in January 1998 — Cleveland OH, Kansas City MO and Houston (Hobby) TX. Three other non-Orlando routes were also started: Boston-Fort Lauderdale, Columbus OH-Tampa and Washington DC (Dulles)-Tampa. These new services take the total flights-per-day to 144 and the

Below: *On approach to Houston's Hobby airport in June 1996 is Delta Boeing 737-232 N305DL, bearing the Olympic Games titling on the forward fuselage. This aircraft was one of the 25 737-200s redeployed to the Delta Express operation at Orlando in October 1996.* Geoffrey P. Jones

number of cities served by Delta Express to 14. Paulette Corbin, who is now Delta Express' Managing Director, says that they are continually looking at new markets as they believe there is a lot more business available in the US for this type of service. She did however, rule out an operation from the gambling cities of Las Vegas and Atlantic City. Sadly, the demise of ValuJet probably helped to buoy up Delta Express's success in the Florida market. It also gave Delta Express the opportunity to highlight its safety pedigree to sceptical customers who wanted to know 'everything' about low-cost airlines following the ValuJet crash.

In the first year of operation, Delta Express load factors (the percentage of seats sold/occupied against total seat capacity) averaged 71% and are now believed to have risen to around 75%, slightly above the 73% figure being quoted for mainline Delta. By the end of October 1996 load factors were 78.5% against a forecast of 65% and have regularly exceeded forecasts ever since. A 95% load factor was the record to date, established in November 1997. Turnround goal-time on a flight is 30min and Delta Express is regularly achieving 27min or less. Whilst the flight attendants sport the casual Delta Express leisure image, the pilots continue to wear regular uniforms. Feedback from employees is always appreciated — it was a pilot who suggested that small time and cost savings could be made at the airport by taxying the aircraft in on its left-hand engine only. This enabled the ramp staff to get to the baggage (the baggage doors are on the right-hand side of the aircraft) and the aircraft more quickly without having to wait for the engine to spool down. The aircraft is then taxied out on the right engine only to keep the accumulated hours for the engine pair the same. This innovation from Delta Express has now been adopted by mainline Delta, just the sort of 'concept from the front line' that Delta Air Lines' new CEO Leo Mullin likes.

Profits for Delta Express are not available and not reported separately, being assimilated into the main airline's figures. 'Skip' Barnette revealed that the first three months of Delta Express operations 'far exceeded financial expectations, [and] that we've done a lot of things very well'. However, it is publicly stated that Delta Express is a highly productive operation, one of the largest revenue-producing segments of its system and capitalising on the rapid growth of leisure travel. Profitability was confirmed from the first day of the Delta Express operation, forming a significant part of Delta's $11,096 million domestic operating revenue and $1,242 million operating income during 1997 and helping these figures on their steady annual increase.

Right: *N4513W Boeing 737-247 in the classic Western 'swizzle-stick' livery, seen on approach to McCarren Field, Las Vegas, in April 1982.* Geoffrey P. Jones

Above: *The flightdeck of Delta L-1011 TriStar 500 N739DA, preparing for push-back at London's Gatwick Airport in April 1991, prior to a flight to Atlanta.*
Geoffrey P. Jones

Below: *Ramp scene at Atlanta in April 1991with Boeing 767, 757, 737, MD-88 and TriStar aircraft, a scene that has changed very little in the last seven years.*
Geoffrey P. Jones

Above: *Ex-Western Boeing 727-247 N2816W was delivered new in May 1974 and transferred to the Delta fleet following the merger in 1987. The aircraft is pictured at Delta's Salt Lake City hub in January 1995.* Tony Carre.

Below: *'Fly Delta Jets', a huge sign welcomes you on arrival at Atlanta Worldport. Here Boeing 727-247 N831WA in Delta's new livery touches down on runway 27R in March 1998.* Geoffrey P. Jones

Delta Shuttle

Delta Air Lines' Delta Shuttle operation is a legacy of the demise of PanAm in 1991. The history of the shuttle, though, goes back much further and is one of the unique aspects of the US air transport system, a function of history and of geography in what has come to be known as the Northeast Corridor. As a measure of the importance of this market, recent statistics show that the Boston-New York segment is the fourth largest market in the 48 contiguous United States and that Washington-New York is the seventh largest. The shuttle's history can be summarised as follows:

30 April 1961	Eastern Air Lines began shuttle operations between Washington and New York (LaGuardia) and Boston
29 April 1962	New York (Newark) was added to the shuttle network
24 April 1966	Eastern introduced Boeing 727 jet service on shuttle routes
12 February 1967	American Airlines inaugurated New York-Boston service with BAC-111s
Late 1960s	Northeast Airlines inaugurated New York (LaGuardia) service with DC-9-30s and Boeing 727-100s and 200s
Early 1980s	New York Air began service
August 1982	PEOPLExpress started service between New York (Newark) and Washington (National)
1 October 1986	PanAm took over from New York Air with the PanAm shuttle
June 1989	Trump Shuttle inaugurated service with Boeing 727s inherited from Eastern
1 September 1991	Delta Shuttle acquired assets of the PanAm Shuttle along with what remained of PanAm's Atlantic route network for $416 million
1 April 1992	USAir took over Trump Shuttle, now renamed Shuttle Inc
27 February 1997	With USAir's name change, it became US Airways Shuttle

Delta Air Lines' strength in the important northeastern US market came about largely as a result of the May 1972 merger between Delta and Northeast Airlines. With the merger, Delta's fleet of Boeing 727s was further enhanced, with the 13 727-295s of Northeast added to the 14 727-200s that Delta had ordered for delivery from 1972 onwards. Subsequent 727-200 acquisitions brought Delta's fleet of the type to 129 aircraft, at the time the biggest 727 fleet in the world. It was with 14 of these aircraft, dedicated wholly to the Delta Shuttle, that it became established on the Shuttle routes, operating 64 scheduled flights each weekday between Boston, New York and Washington.

Shuttle services have always been known for strong yield and with Delta's standards of service, performance and guaranteed seats, the service continues to attract an increasing percentage of business traffic: 100% despatch reliability is important for the Delta Shuttle because of the nature of the intense competition and demands of its customers. With a small, dedicated fleet, Delta's mechanics can stay on top of any technical problems with these aircraft. If aircraft are not delivered in a 'ready to go condition', then the competition is liable to steal a march on them. Maintenance work is balanced between the Shuttle's three cities, with LaGuardia having more room but Boston having hangarage. The Delta Shuttle has managed to achieve this growth in traffic whilst at the same time significantly reducing operating costs to meet 'Leadership 7.5' objectives.

More than 70% of Delta Shuttle customers take at least four Shuttle flights per year. One of its strong selling points is the guaranteed seat, the concept that a 727 will operate a flight even if only for a single passenger. The reality is that this could

Above: *N928DL MD-88 at the gate at Washington National's North Terminal in June 1990 before Delta started flying the Washington-New York-Boston shuttle, and when Donald Trump's Trump Shuttle was in operation.* Geoffrey P. Jones

happen, but Shuttle Planning and Control, in close liaison with Delta's Special Operations in Atlanta, plan to ensure that it does not. Flights have been initiated for three or four passengers but by the time the aircraft is ready to go, passengers have been added from the next scheduled flight and the load built to 30 or 40 passengers. On an average day the Delta Shuttle will operate 12 to 20 extra sections, most of which are forecast in advance and operated within minutes of the scheduled departure time of the prime flight. An unplanned extra section, known as an 'ad hoc' operates in response to unusual demand, and will operate no later than 15min after the scheduled flight. In 1997 the Delta Shuttle boarded over 2 million passengers (system-wide revenue passengers enplaned in 1997 were 101.147 million) and achieved the boarding milestone of its 10 millionth customer in April 1997. As a measure of Delta's continuing commitment to and investment in its Shuttle it opened its new facilities at Washington National's Terminal B (Gates 18 and 20) on 30 January 1998, putting it adjacent to Delta's mainline operation. The majority of Shuttle passengers travel for business and nearly one half of them live in the New York/New Jersey area. During 1997 an on-time departure rate exceeding 95% was achieved.

Delta Shuttle Facts and Figures

- 64 daily flights between New York and Washington or New York and Boston are scheduled.
- Extra sections are added during peak travel periods.
- Flights depart every hour on the half-hour from 06.30 until 21.30, with the last flight to Washington departing at 21.00.
- At weekends 56 daily flights between New York and Washington or New York and Boston are scheduled.
- Weekend schedules are a departure every hour on the half-hour from 07.30 until 20.30 on a Saturday and from 08.30 until 21.30 on a Sunday.
- Customer breakdown: 80% travel for business, 36% take four to 12 trips per year, 35% take 13 or more trips per year and 42% live in the New York/New Jersey area.
- More than 10 million passengers have flown on the Delta Shuttle since September 1991.

Above: *Sporting the new Delta Shuttle livery is N412DA, one of the 14 dedicated Shuttle Boeing 727-232s that fly the intense schedules between Boston, New York (LaGuardia) and Washington (National).* Delta Air Lines

Below: *The vast acres of San Francisco International Airport in May 1990 with N400DA Boeing 727-232 at the gate and a Boeing 757 under tow beyond.* Geoffrey P. Jones

Above: *Arriving at the gate on Concourse 'A' at Atlanta during a morning 'bank' in April 1991, Boeing 727-232 N475DA slips alongside Boeing 737-232 N302DL, which has since been transferred to the Orlando-based Delta Express fleet.* Geoffrey P. Jones

Below: *N303DL, one of 26 Boeing 737-232s dedicated to the Orlando-based Delta Express fleet, the airline's low-cost, low-frills subsidiary that has been flying since 1 October 1996.* Delta Air Lines

- Boarding milestones:

one million	April 1992
two million	October 1992
four million	February 1994
six million	March 1995
eight million	April 1996
10 million	April 1997

- an average of 150,000 customers are boarded per month.
- Delta Shuttle guarantees a seat which means that if a regularly scheduled flight fills up before departure time, then Delta guarantees that it will roll out another Delta Shuttle aircraft.
- overall on-time departure performance rating exceeds 95%.
- Delta Shuttle aircraft fleet numbers 14 Boeing 727-232s with a customer-seating capacity of 157 in luxury leather seats.
- Delta Shuttle crews consist of three flight deck and four cabin staff.
- in-flight amenities include healthy snacks, GTE Airfones, 4in more leg-room than the average airline seats, complimentary wine, gourmet coffee, beer and other beverages.
- a Delta Water Shuttle provides quick ground connection between LaGuardia and Manhattan, with alternative stops at 62nd Street, 34th Street and Wall Street.
- reservations are not required for the Delta Shuttle, automatic ticketing machines being located at the main departure airports — dedicated customer facilities are located at New York's Marine Air Terminal, Boston Logan and Washington National. Reservations can be made for the Delta Shuttle if required.
- Delta Shuttle has its own web site at HYPERLINK http://www.delta-air.com/shuttle www.delta-air.com/shuttle.

Below: *Boeing 727-232 N507DA lifts off at Atlanta Worldport in March 1998.*
Geoffrey P. Jones

Affiliated Companies — The Delta Connection

ASA — Atlantic Southeast Airlines

On 1 May 1984 Atlantic Southeast Airlines (ASA) entered into a code-share agreement with Delta Air Lines. This enabled ASA to use Delta's International Air Transport Association (IATA) two-letter 'DL' designator. The DL is used in reservations, timetables, ticketing, schedules, tariffs, legal and other airline industry applications. ASA also has its own IATA two-letter code: 'EV'.

ASA was established in Atlanta in March 1979 and flew its first service in July. Its first flights were between Atlanta and Columbus, Macon and Athens with up to five services a day between Atlanta and Columbus using a small fleet of DHC-6 Twin Otters and EMB-110 Bandeirantes. It became a public company in 1983, by which time its fleet had grown to 17 aircraft, including five DHC-7 Dash Seven aircraft, serving 21 cities in Georgia, Alabama, Mississippi, Tennessee, North and South Carolina and northern Florida.

ASA now operates as a Delta Connection airline from both Delta's Atlanta and Dallas/Fort Worth hubs serving the cities and towns that generate smaller traffic levels. Rio Airways also joined as a Delta Connection at Dallas/Fort Worth in June 1984, which was at the time one of the US's largest commuter airlines and operated a mixed fleet of 27 aircraft that included DHC-6s, 7s and 8s, Super King Air 200s and SA226 Metro IIs. They were later assimilated into ASA when Rio went into bankruptcy in December 1986.
ASA's current Chairman and CEO is George Pickett, Jr, and President is John Beiser. Delta owns a 20% shareholding in ASA and as with many of the world's franchised operators, its aircraft now wear the colours of the franchiser: Delta on the fuselage but with ASA's colours on the aircraft's tail. There are currently 2,500 ASA employees and 80 aircraft in the fleet — 63 EMB-120 Brasilias, 12 ATR-72s — and by spring 1998 10 out of the total of 30

Below: *Increasing numbers of Canadair RJ-100s are now being flown by Delta Connection airlines, including Atlanta-based Atlantic Southeast Airlines. N828AS is seen here newly delivered at Atlanta in March 1998.* Geoffrey P. Jones

Above: *'Not too revolutionary' was one of the comments about the new Landor-designed Delta colour scheme introduced in 1997 and sported here by Boeing 757-232 N604DL. Delta's previous colour scheme had been in use for over 35 years.* Geoffrey P. Jones

Below: *Brand-new and never having carried a paying passenger, N199DN Boeing 767-332ER is seen in the paint shop at Atlanta's TOC being finished and fitted out in March 1998 ready to enter commercial service.* Geoffrey P. Jones

Above: *Engine access cowling raised around one of the two 120,000lb (48,000hp) thrust Pratt & Whitney PW4060 engines fitted to one of Delta's Boeing 767-332ERs during an inspection at Atlanta's TOC.* Geoffrey P. Jones

Below: *Delta Air Lines Boeing 767-232 N102DA Spirit of Delta, purchased by Delta employees in 1983 through wage cuts and other cost-saving measures when the airline's finances were precarious. Pictured at Atlanta in March 1998, still proudly wearing the name.* Geoffrey P. Jones

Left: *Atlanta-based Atlantic Southeast Airlines operated a small fleet of De Havilland Canada DHC-7s in the late 1980s and early 1990s as part of its Delta Connection. N721AS is seen here at Atlanta in April 1991.*
Geoffrey P. Jones

Canadair RJ-100-2B19s that ASA has on order had arrived. All DHC-7s and the five leased BAe146s that ASA operated have all been disposed of. The airline had envisaged a fleet of up to 20 146s but changed tack after operating them for two years to standardise on a fleet of ATR-72s and Canadair RJ-100s.

ASA is second only to Delta Air Lines itself in Atlanta and serves both the Atlanta and Dallas markets with over 557 flights a day to 57 cities.

Comair

Established in Cincinnati in 1977 by David Mueller and his father Raymond Mueller, Comair Holdings was formed in 1979 and became a public company in July 1981. Comair became a Delta Connection airline on 1 September 1984. As with ASA, it was able to use the 'DL' IATA two-letter designator as well as its own 'OH' designator. Comair's first scheduled services were from Cincinnati to Akron, Dayton, Columbus and Cleveland (Ohio), Detroit (Michigan) and Indianapolis; equipment in the early 1980s was mainly Piper PA-31 Navajo and Navajo Chieftain aircraft, along with the airline's first Embraer EMB-110 Bandeirantes.

By 1985 virtually all of Comair's PA-31s had been replaced by larger aircraft, including EMB-110s, SF-340s, Swearingen SA227 Metro IIIs and Shorts SD-330s. They were serving a large number of smaller communities in the US midwest from Cincinnati, as well as more southern destinations in Tennessee and Alabama. Establishment of a second Comair hub centred on Orlando, Florida, occurred in 1990, coinciding with the airline's order for EMB-120 Brasilias.

David Mueller, the airline's founder, is still Chairman and CEO of Comair, with David Siebenburgen the President and Chief Operations Officer, the headquarters still being at Cincinnati. Delta Air Lines has a 23% shareholding in Comair. The two main operations centres, providing feed from many smaller cities into the main Delta Air Lines network, are at Cincinnati and Orlando. Comair employs 3,200 and has a fleet of 92 aircraft (39 EMB-120 Brasilias and 53 Canadair RJ-100s) which retain the Comair colours. The airline currently offers 652 daily departures serving 80 cities from its Cincinnati and Orlando hubs.

BEX Business Express

Business Express was formed at Hartford, Connecticut, and started charter services in 1981. Its first scheduled commuter airline services to many of the mid- and small-sized communities in New England started in November 1984. At about the same time (1 May 1984) Ransom Airlines of Philadelphia had entered a code-share agreement with Delta Air Lines, having earlier had a similar agreement with Allegheny Airlines before it became USAir. Ransom Airlines operated the Delta code-share until the airline's owner, J. Dawson Ransom, sold out to PanAm in June 1986. Business Express joined Delta in July 1986 as a Delta Connection airline, having just bought out Pilgrim Airlines, which in turn

Above: *Delta Connection airline Comair is based in Cincinnati and has now replaced its Saab 340 fleet with EMB-120s and Canadair RJ-100s. This Saab 340, N360CA, is pictured at Detroit in October 1987.* Tony Carre

had just bought Newair. Pilgrim was operating DHC-6 Twin Otters and F-27 Friendships from New York JFK and LaGuardia, Boston and Washington DC. Newair had also served many smaller communities in New England as well as New York's Newark and LaGuardia airports, and Philadelphia, using a fleet of DHC-6 Twin Otters, EMB-110 Bandeirantes and Shorts SD-360s.

When Business Express became a Delta Connection airline in July 1986 it too was able to use the 'DL' two-letter IATA designator as well as retaining its own two-letter code, 'HQ'. In March 1995 Business Express announced its expansion at Boston/Logan airport, enabling it to operate 80% of its 158 daily flights from there using a renovated terminal site. Business Express also became a Northwest Airlink commuter operator for Northwest Airlines. In January 1996 Business Express filed for Chapter 11 bankruptcy protection and returned three Avro RJ-70s it had been operating.

With Robert Martens as its Chairman and CEO and Gary Ellmer as President and Chief Operating Officer, Business Express's headquarters are at Dover, New Hampshire, and it now employs 1,100, mostly at its three main hubs — New York LaGuardia and JFK airports and Boston/Logan airport. Its fleet centres around 39 Saab 340A and 340B aircraft as well as BAe Jetstream 31s and Raytheon Beechcraft 1900Cs. Business Express is now claimed to be the largest regional carrier in the northeast US and from its three main hubs offers over 340 daily departures to 24 cities. Its importance at JFK has increased dramatically in the last year as Delta Air Lines has developed international routes here as a partial substitute for its former European hub at Frankfurt.

SkyWest Airlines

SkyWest Airlines was established at St George Municipal airport, Utah, in March 1972, operating charter services, air-freight, air ambulance and flight training with a fleet of single-engined Cessnas. Scheduled services from the cities of Salt Lake City, Pocatello, Milford, Delta, Richfield, Fillmore, Cedar City and St George, all in Utah, were supplemented by services to cities in Nevada and Arizona as well as sightseeing flights to natural wonders in the area such as the Grand Canyon. Piper PA-31 Navajo Chieftains were used initially for these services, supplemented by Swearingen SA226 Metro IIs and EMB-110

Above: *Spirit of Delta was one of two of Delta Air Lines aircraft painted in a special scheme to help mark the 1996 Olympic Games in Atlanta. Delta was a major sponsor and the official airline of the Games.* Delta Air Lines

Below: *The first aircraft to be painted in Delta Air Lines new Landor-designed livery, in April 1997, was Boeing 767-332 N190DN.* Delta Air Lines

Above: *Boeing 767-332ER N196DN, which first flew at Boeing's Everett/Paine Field on 23 October 1997 and was delivered to Atlanta in Delta's new livery in November, seen here nosed in to the jetway at Atlanta Worldport's international Concourse 'E' in March 1998.* Geoffrey P. Jones

Below: *N892DL, one of two MD-11s leased by Delta in 1990-1 prior to the delivery of its own in 1991.* Delta Air Lines

Bandeirantes. In 1984 SkyWest Airlines absorbed Sun Aire Lines, together with its fleet of 11 Swearingen SA226TC Metro IIs and its scheduled network based on Palm Springs, California. Sun Aire had been formed as Borrego Springs Airlines in November 1968 and began operations on 22 December 1968 with a single Cessna 402 twin. Sun Aire Lines developed an extensive commuter network serving many communities in the Los Angeles basin but spreading as far east as Yuma and Phoenix in Arizona.

When Delta Air Lines acquired Western Air Lines on 1 April 1987, it inherited the commuter airline operating as Western Express. This was assimilated into the operations of SkyWest Airlines and in turn SkyWest signed a marketing and code-share agreement with Delta Air Lines in 1987 allowing the 'DL' two-letter IATA designator to be used for Delta Connection flights. SkyWest's own two-letter IATA designator is 'OO'. Delta Air Lines now has a 20% shareholding in SkyWest Airlines.

The fleet is centred around the Swearingen/Fairchild SA227 Metro III and the Embraer EMB-120 Brasilia. Deliveries of the order for 10 Canadair RJ-100s has now been completed. The Metro IIIs have been retired. SkyWest was also the launch customer for the Embraer EMB-210 Brasilia Advanced.

Jerry Atkins is SkyWest's President and CEO, with Ron Reber as Executive Vice President and Chief Operations Officer and there are 2,100 employees. Still based at St George in Utah, SkyWest's two main hubs are Salt Lake City and Los Angeles International (LAX), with a smaller hub at Portland, Oregon. SkyWest Airlines now offers more daily departures from LAX than any other airline, serving eight western states with over 294 flights daily to 48 cities.

Trans States Airlines

In early 1998, St Louis, Missouri-based Trans States Airlines signed a tentative agreement with Delta Air Lines to operate as a Delta Connection carrier at New York JFK. Business Express, which currently provides Delta Connection services at JFK will continue, but will now concentrate on Boston and LaGuardia.

Trans States was formed as Resort Air in May 1982 and signed a marketing agreement with USAir in November 1993. It currently serves more than 30 cities in 10 US states with a fleet of ATR-42s and 72s, BAe Jetstream 32s and 41s and EMB-120 Brasilias. Its IATA two-letter designator is '9N' and it has recently been operating commuter services for TWA as TW Express as well as for USAir (now US Airways).

Left: *SkyWest EMB-120 Brasilia N204SW taxying for departure at Fresno, California, in June 1994, one of the 48 cities in the eight western US states that this Delta Connection airline serves.*
Geoffrey P. Jones

Below: *Activity on the Comair (Delta Connection) ramp at Orlando in April 1995. Two EMB-120 Brasilias and two Swearingen SA227AC Metro IIIs.* Geoffrey P. Jones

Below: *Business Express (BEX) Saab 340A N350BE at New York's JFK in April 1993. Business Express is a Delta Connection operator and also serves Delta at New York/LaGuardia and Boston airports.* Geoffrey P. Jones

Above: *Being prepared for departure from London's Gatwick Airport for the daily service to Delta's hub at Cincinnati, is MD-11 N803DE. The MD-11 replaced the L-1011-500 TriStar on transatlantic services.* Geoffrey P. Jones

Below: *One of the two aircraft painted in the special Delta Olympic livery for the 1996 Atlanta Olympic Games, N6202S, which became N812DE after delivery.* Delta Air Lines

Above: *Delta's two current (1998) widebodied trijets together at Atlanta Worldport: an L-1011 TriStar taxying and an MD-11 just rolling off Atlanta's runway 27R.* Geoffrey P. Jones

Below: *Delta originally used the old South Terminal finger at London's Gatwick Airport before moving to the newly opened North Terminal in 1994. Here N1738D, an L-1011-250, and N751DA, an L-1011-500, can be seen at Gatwick in April 1991. Aircraft used by Delta on international services can be distinguished by the US flag on the tip of the tail.* Geoffrey P. Jones

Delta's Hubs

Atlanta Worldport

Known until recently as Atlanta Hartsfield International Airport, Atlanta is Delta Air Lines most important hub — its operational base and corporate headquarters. Early in 1998 Delta added new domestic frequencies from Atlanta Worldport to Seattle, San Francisco and Sarasota. In March 1998 the airline offered 621 flights and more than 105,000 seats daily from Atlanta Worldport. These figures will increase even more as Delta's new Latin American and Japanese services commence during the spring and summer of 1998. These statistics do not include the Delta Connector flights of Atlantic Southeast Airlines.

Delta's Atlanta Worldport ranks as the world's largest single-hub carrier operation. Delta operates from all five ('A', 'B', 'C', 'D' and 'E') concourses at Atlanta, the 'A' Concourse operation alone being the second largest airline operation in the world. Concourse 'E' is for international flights. These concourses are interlinked by an underground train system. The airport at Atlanta is owned by the City of Atlanta, Delta leasing the facilities to operate 80 out of the total 105 gates available on the five concourses and with 5,000 employees assigned to working out on the ramp.

Overseeing the whole minute-by-minute operation of Delta is its Airport Control Center (ACC), which in turn is linked with the Operations Control Center (OCC) (see separate chapter). The OCC plans and the ACC operates, based in a special control tower on top of Concourse 'B' and with a subsidiary control tower on 'D'. From these one can physically see ramp operations, taking over from the FAA the operations control of the aircraft on the ramp when an aircraft leaves or approaches a taxi-way.

The newly appointed Vice President of Atlanta Worldport in 1998 is W. E. 'Skip' Barnette, former Vice President of Delta Express. He believes that the airport works well, but if a problem occurs, very often due to weather, then decisions have to be made on how to 'bounce the system back'. He believes the objective is to try to make the operation more efficient, but likens Delta's Atlanta Worldport to a factory: 'You have people, bags, cargo, mail and aeroplanes — we have to process them through and out the other end. Most of the time we're just looking and operating what goes on inside the factory but there are other things outside which impinge on our operations, air traffic control and weather being the two most frequent. We can't improve or alter air traffic control, which is not slot restricted but is flow restricted. We certainly can't

Left: *Atlanta Worldport with N468DA Boeing 727-232 at push-back, a Boeing 757 taxying out and a Boeing 727-232 departing off runway 27R.*
Geoffrey P. Jones

alter the weather but by being aware of what is likely to happen, combined with what is happening at present, we can make planned decisions on how best to prepare for adverse weather and deal with it. All the time we are trying to run Delta's Atlanta Worldport in the most efficient manner, to achieve on-scheduled departures and arrivals for our 105,000 daily seat departures.'

Delta's Atlanta Worldport operation and its three other main hubs work on up to as many as seven main waves of arriving and departing aircraft during the day, referred to by Delta as 'banks'. Between these 'banks' and at the quieter night-time between 23.00 and 06.00 the airport's facilities are not maximised. There is always a dilemma between trying to flatten out these 'banks' yet optimising the scheduling department's requirement for the maximum of connecting flight possibilities. At present optimum connection time on interline or connecting flights is 90min between a flight docking at a gate on arrival, the passsenger and his/her baggage changing to the departing flight and the commencement of push-back from the docking gate. On international flights, immigration — which can take as long as 45min — is one of the biggest obstacles to Delta's achievement of this 90min target.

Atlanta Worldport has four parallel runways, aligned 09/27, the longest being 11,889ft (3,624m). From these Delta — the other airlines using Atlanta — manages to handle more flights per day than Dallas/Fort Worth with its six runways. The biggest challenge that Delta faces at Atlanta Worldport in 1998 is the advent of the airline's new Latin American services as, historically, flights entering the US from Latin America have had a higher number of rejected passenger entries than from any other part of the world (due to irregularities with visas and other paperwork). Delta will be studying these problems in order to fulfil its commitment to all its passengers and judge what effect they might have on the company's operations overall.

In only three years since 1970 has Delta's Enplanement traffic declined at Atlanta, in 1981 and 1982 and 1990. A summary of the figures is as follows: Delta Air Lines currently (1 April 1998) offers 620 daily flights from Atlanta Worldport to 120 worldwide destinations, out of a system-wide total of 2,701 flights.

Year	Enplanements	Growth	Departures	Growth
1970	4,090,732	-	71,291	-
1975	6,367,863	55.7%	82,497	15.7%
1980	10,526,821	65.3%	120,249	45.8%
1985	10,886,409	3.4%	131,169	9.1%
1990	13,099,910	20.3%	153,765	17.2%
1995	20,768,258	58.5%	208,050	33.3%
1997	26,000,000 (approx)	25.2%	236,155	13.5%

Cincinnati/Northern Kentucky International

Cincinnati (ICAO three-letter code CVG) is Delta Air Lines' second largest hub in terms of the number of daily flight departures, now totalling 218, seven of which are international flights. In addition to these, Comair, the Delta Connection airline, has more than 240 flights daily; between them, Delta and Comair account for almost 90% of all flights at Cincinnati. As much as 80% of all Americans live within an 800-mile radius of Cincinnati. Delta first served the city in 1941 with a service from Savannah in Georgia and started to develop Cincinnati as a hub in 1981 when it operated 30 flights a day from five gates and flew 1,026,464 passengers. Growth has been considerable since then:

Above: *An L-1011-500 TriStar lifts off from Atlanta Worldport's runway 27L, framed by a taxying Delta B.767-232 in March 1998.* Geoffrey P. Jones

Below: *N186SW Embraer EMB-120 Brasilia ER of Delta Connection SkyWest Airlines (which has a fleet of 50 Brasilias with another 20 on order) pictured at Salt Lake City in January 1995 on the first day of operations of SkyWest's dedicated commuter terminal there.* Tony Carre

Above: *Preparing for departure from Detroit in October 1987, Comair Swearingen SA227 Metro III N3116F. Comair became a Delta Connection airline in September 1984.* Tony Carre

Below: *Providing feed into Delta's Dallas/Fort Worth hub is Delta Connection airline Atlantic Southeast Airlines (ASA). One of its AI(R) ATR-72s, N643AS, is seen taxying in at Dallas in January 1995.* Tony Carre

Year	Enplanements	Growth	No of daily flights
1980	534,818	-	30
1985	958,048	79%	45
1990	3,307,732	245%	145
1995	5,487,043	65.9%	220
1997	7,143,890	30.2%	218

In 1994 Delta opened a new $375 million terminal with two concourses which added 50 new gates to the airport's facilities. The airline currently offers direct transatlantic and international services from Cincinnati to Brussels, Frankfurt, London, Montreal, Paris and Zurich — the Zurich flights being operated on a code-share basis but by a Delta crew and with Delta aircraft.

Dallas/Fort Worth

Dallas/Fort Worth (ICAO three-letter code DFW) is Delta Air Lines' fourth largest hub with 131 daily flight departures. It operates from 27 gates to 41 destinations nonstop, carrying 5,018,540 passengers from here in 1997. The main runway is aligned at 16/34 and is 12,000ft (3,658m) in length.

Salt Lake City

Western Air Lines first started its mail service from Salt Lake City on 17 April 1926 and its first passenger service on 23 May 1926. Delta began its first service to Salt Lake City on 28 April 1980, during a period when passenger boardings at the airport for all airlines were growing at a rate of 8.5% annually. On the 1987 Delta takeover of Western it immediately became Delta's third largest hub. Delta now provides air services to more than 65% of Salt Lake City's passengers. In addition, the Salt Lake City-based Delta Connection airline, SkyWest Airlines, offers 87 flights daily to 26 destinations nonstop, Delta and SkyWest together now operating over 70% of flights at Salt Lake City. Every month there Delta boards an average of over 500,000 passengers with over 25,000 flights annually.

New York (John F. Kennedy)

New York's John F. Kennedy International Airport (ICAO three-letter code JFK) is growing rapidly, being Delta Air Lines' fifth largest hub with 45 daily flight departures. The airline operates from 28 gates, flying nonstop to 37 destinations (including 103 international transatlantic and Mexico flights every week). With code-sharing flights included, the number of weekly Delta international departures out of JFK is 200. Delta flights (excluding code-sharing flights) accounted for 2,362,865 passengers at JFK in 1997, the year in which Delta celebrated 40 years of service here — the original schedules were two daily DC-7 flights on 15 May 1957 to Atlanta and to Dallas. The 1972 Delta merger with Northeast Airlines gave Delta important access from JFK to several important New England and Florida destinations.

The main runway at JFK is aligned at 13/31 and is 14,572ft (4,441m) in length. It has been a leading US gateway to Europe since the start of practical transatlantic flights, now handling an estimated 40% of all traffic between the US and Europe. With the running down of Delta's Frankfurt hub, there has been a parallel increase in the importance attached to its JFK hub, building on its position as the number one transatlantic US airline. Passenger feed into JFK has been supplied by the Delta Connection airline, Business Express (BEX), although this status is currently (April 1998) in flux with BEX reportedly concentrating on serving Boston and New York (LaGuardia), leaving JFK to be served by Trans States Airlines (see separate chapter). All Delta and Delta Connection flights operate from Terminal 3 at JFK.

Atlanta, Georgia

No of gates	No of employees	No of daily flights	No of nonstop destinations	Passengers (end Dec '97)
97	27,926*	620**	120	23,894,884

Cincinnati, Ohio

No of gates	No of employees	No of daily flights	No of nonstop destinations	Passengers (end Dec '97)
50	4,500*	221**	73**	7,143,890

Dallas/Fort Worth, Texas

No of gates	No of employees	No of daily flights	No of nonstop destinations	Passengers (end Dec '97)
27	4,984*	131**	41**	5,018,540

John F. Kennedy, New York

No of gates	No of employees	No of daily flights	No of nonstop destinations	Passengers (end Dec '97)
28	3,897*	45**	37**	2,362,865

Salt Lake City, Utah

No of gates	No of employees	No of daily flights	No of nonstop destinations	Passengers (end Dec '97)
32	4,379*	168**	49**	7,241,631

*As of 1 March 1998
**Effective 1 April 1998

Below: *With Delta Boeing 727 tails beyond, MD-88 N940DL decelerates after landing at Atlanta Worldport in March 1998.* Geoffrey P. Jones

Above: *Delta Connection carrier Comair operates mainly into hubs at Cincinnati and Orlando. Here one of its 39 Embraer EMB-120 Brasilias — N179CA — is seen preparing for a late evening flight from Orlando to Miami in April1991.* Geoffrey P. Jones

Below: *Painting by Brad Driggers of Delta's Ship 41 (NC28241), its first DC-3 to enter commercial service in December 1940, flying over the old Atlanta Hartsfield airport.* Geoffrey P. Jones

Above: *Lovingly restored and still flying in 1998 with a group of enthusiasts in the old Northeast Airlines colours, Douglas DC-3 N33623 (s/n 3288) is one of the first three delivered to the airline in May 1941.* D. Story

Below: *N811DE MD-11 at Gatwick's North Terminal in March 1998, being readied for the daily 09.45 departure on the 9hr 20min direct flight to Atlanta Worldport.* Geoffrey P. Jones

Above: *Delta has always had a strong presence in the US northeast, strengthened by the takeover of Northeast Airlines in 1972. Here a mix of Delta types can be seen at its New York (JFK) hub in April 1993, Boeing 727-232 N466DA is in the foreground.* Geoffrey P. Jones

Above: *Delta Air Lines' domination at New York JFK in April 1993: the scene includes several ex-PanAm Airbus A310s, one of them being N813PA.*
Geoffrey P. Jones

Delta's Global Partners

No major world airline in the late 1990s is without its 'partners'. These range from full-blown alliances with each airline having equity stakes in the other, such as Northwest Airlines and KLM, to the more basic code-share agreement on a specific route. As the proposed alliance between British Airways and American Airlines awaits ratification and United Airlines' 'Star Alliance' grouping grows more substantial, other major world airlines such as Delta Air Lines have not been left standing. Such alliances are now taken for granted although they are really very 'young' in airline terms, having only been consummated in the last 10 years.

It was a major snub to Delta when its discussions during 1997 with Continental Airlines about a major merger foundered. Talks between Continental's Gordon Bethune and Delta's Leo Mullin were apparently precipitated in 1996 by American's interest in US Airways. It appeared that Delta and Continental '...should fit together' according to Continental's Bethune when talks between the two airlines were close to an agreement in August 1997. In February 1998 the 'merger' was declared to be off and Continental agreed to a strategic alliance with Northwest Airlines. It is reported that concerns over labour and the retention of some of Continental's top executives scuttled the planned merger.

Not discouraged, Delta Air Lines, buoyant from the news that its 1997 passenger figures were the best ever on record and that for the first time in the airline's history it had carried more than 100 million passengers in one calendar year (in fact 103,295,376), got on with the business of cementing alliances with its existing and possible new partners. But Delta has not ruled out possible mergers with other US carriers if conditions and terms are correct, United Airlines being the prime candidate.

Most airlines that fly the North Atlantic are awaiting the outcome of the US-European Bilateral Agreement and of almost equal significance and closely linked with the bilateral, are the BA/AA merger plans. Delta has had detailed talks with Air France but failure of the December 1997 round of talks between France and the US prevented this commercial agreement being signed. Mark Drusch, Delta's Vice President of Marketing Development, confirmed in March 1998 that Delta was keen to sign with Air France but that it all hinged on the signing of the bilateral agreement. Delta Air Lines has already made a first step into France with its purchase of a 34% stake in the Lyon-based regional carrier Proteus Airlines which it is assisting with an 18-month operational planning exercise. This is the first time that a US major has taken a share of a French airline and Proteus will soon have the largest European fleet of Raytheon Beechcraft 1900s (Cs and Ds) and is the launch customer for the Fairchild Dornier 328JET.

WORLDWIDE PARTNERS
Aer Lingus
AeroMexico
Austrian Airlines
Finnair
Korean Air
Malev Hungarian Airlines
sabena
swissair
tap Air Portugal
Trans Brasil

Above: *Ex-PanAm N510PA L-1011-500 TriStar, now Delta's N760DH, powered by its three Rolls-Royce RB.211 engines, seen taxying for take-off at Atlanta Worldport in March 1998.* Geoffrey P. Jones

Below: *A short-fuselage Boeing 767-232, N115DA, one of the original 15 767s delivered to Delta in the 1980s, is seen on approach to Miami in April 1991.* Geoffrey P. Jones

In 1989 Delta, Singapore Airlines and Swissair formed a Global Excellence Alliance (GEA), and in November 1990 the three airlines announced a trilateral purchase of equity between the three partners from the open market to a maximum of 5% of each other's stock. Since 8 April 1997 an Open Skies Agreement has been in effect. Strongest of the current Delta alliances is that with Swissair, of which it owns 4.6%. Swissair-operated flights with DL code-share are flown from Zurich to Atlanta, New York (JFK), Los Angeles, Chicago, Boston, Philadelphia, Washington DC and Cincinnati; they also fly from Geneva to New York (JFK). Closely following the Swissair alliance is the partnership with Singapore Airlines, Delta owning a 2.7% shareholding in Singapore. The most significant Singapore-operated flight with DL code-share is New York JFK-Singapore. Singapore Airlines has notified Delta of its intent to remain a bilateral partner instead of joining Delta's alliances — meetings are in progress to revisit antitrust immunity between the US and Singapore. Delta is also hopeful that Singapore Airlines will not leave its GEA for the rival Star Alliance (which includes United Airlines and Lufthansa).

Delta's other worldwide partners at March 1998 were Aer Lingus, Aeromexico, Austrian Airlines, Finnair, Korean Air, Malev-Hungarian Airlines, Sabena, TAP-Air Portugal and TransBrasil. Many of the European partners operate their DL code-share flights to New York JFK. Delta has also filed an application to code-share with China Southern and expanded code-share arrangements with Korean Air but both of these are subject to government approval. Delta terminated its code-share agreement with Brazilian airline Varig in 1997 when the Brazilian carrier announced that it was to link with United and Star Alliance.

Delta Air Lines took a planned and reasoned step in late 1997 towards expanding its services into Central and South America, attempting to turn its Atlanta Worldport hub into a major gateway for Latin American air travel. New nonstop services from Atlanta to Costa Rica, El Salvador, Guatemala and Panama started on 5 April 1998. Delta is also seeking authority to serve Argentina, Belize, Bolivia, Colombia, Ecuador, Paraguay and Uruguay. It had already submitted applications to serve Chile and Peru as well as Venezuela, and add a New York JFK-São Paolo service. In March 1998 it was announced that Delta, as part of this growing strategic effort to build its presence in South America, had agreed to acquire a 35% stake in Aeroperu and enter into a 10-year marketing agreement. Delta's stake would match that of Aeromexico and both airlines will now be represented on Aeroperu's board of directors. Government approval will be required for the marketing agreement but Delta started a Atlanta Worldport-Lima service on 1 July 1998. In what is seen as a related move, Delta and Aeromexico have also announced plans to expand on their current marketing agreement.

As Mark Drusch of Delta says: 'We are looking at developing a lot of alliances all over the world — we will talk to any airline, anywhere.'

Right: *Saab 340A N342CA of Delta Connection airline Comair on one of its few international flights outside the USA, seen at Toronto International airport in August 1989.* Geoffrey P. Jones

Delta Maintenance

With Delta Air Lines' aircraft fleet numbering some 555-plus aircraft (excluding those of Delta Connection airlines), the task of keeping these both safely maintained and fully operational on a worldwide basis is massive. A total of approximately 9,000 personnel work in the airline's Technical Operations Division system-wide, representing nearly 20% of the airline's total workforce.

There are four primary maintenance centres within mainland USA, coinciding with Delta's main hubs, as follows:

Atlanta, Georgia	5,500 personnel
Dallas/ Fort Worth, Texas	579 personnel
Cincinnati, Ohio	197 personnel
Salt Lake City, Utah	144 personnel
Other bases worldwide	2,598 personnel

These personnel can be categorised according to the essential tasks they perform, the vast majority are involved in maintenance, of the remainder, 2.9% are in engineering, 3.1% in inspection and 4.4% in material support. At each of the four main bases — and some of the smaller out-stations — Delta maintenance staff work closely with officials of the FAA (Federal Aviation Administration), and aircraft and engine manufacturers. In the latter two categories there are staff on permanent secondment to Delta from companies such as Boeing and Pratt & Whitney.

The Atlanta Worldport facility is by far Delta's biggest maintenance facility with its 5,500 personnel working in the 63-acre (2.7 million sq ft) Technical Operations Center (TOC). Surrounding this vast main building, which consists of hangarage, spray facilities, workshops, engine and equipment shops and offices, is a further 151 acres (6.6 million sq ft) of aprons and parking lots. An annexe (the North Hangar — the former Eastern Air Lines hangar) has recently been added to TOC's capacity. The first hangar, TOC-1 is 600ft long, 250ft wide and 85ft high — TOC-2 is 1,600ft long, 300ft wide and 93ft high (TOC-2 is one of the world's largest cantilevered buildings). TOC-3 is the three separate paint hangars with a ceiling height of 93ft.

The Delta TOC's main maintenance hangar is the focus of all its maintenance operations at Atlanta. It contains 16 aircraft bays, aircraft being slotted in alternately nose to tail, and can accommodate every current type in Delta's fleet. A total of 2,380 hangar personnel keep the TOC functioning on a three-shift, 24hr-a-day basis — the hangar mechanics are classified according to their speciality: base maintenance, sheet metal, aircraft, avionics, hydraulics and cabin skills, for example.

There are seven main levels of aircraft check that Delta performs, ranging from the routine daily pre-trip check to the heavy maintenance visit (HMV), the most in-depth inspection an aircraft ever receives. Delta performs an HMV on each of its aircraft every four to eight years, depending on the aircraft type, and currently in an average year completes 76 HMVs.

The duration and frequency of the following checks are developed through aircraft and engine manufacturers and FAA recommendations in conjunction with Delta's experience of reliability. Using the Boeing 767-300ER as an example, a trip check would take about 30min, whereas an HMV would be performed every eight years, utilize approximately 13,500 man-hours in a Tech Ops facility and take approximately 21 days to complete.

- Trip checks — line mechanics on the main airport ramp conduct a general 'walk-around' inspection.
- Overwater flight check — (where applicable) line and avionics mechanics check oil and other fluids, tyres, brakes, lights, engine computers, cargo equipment, safety equipment and log book items. This check is currently exclusive to Boeing 767-300ER aircraft (Boeing 777s will become liable for this check

upon delivery) for ETOPS or Extended-Range Twin-Engined Operations aircraft, and only ETOPS-qualified maintenance personnel may perform this check. As an ETOPS-rated aircraft, the Boeing 767-300ER can operate up to 180min in flight time from a suitable diversionary airport during long-haul overwater flights.

- Layover check — line and avionics mechanics conduct the above checks in detail, plus additional tasks, including some time-controlled work items. During this check, mechanics inspect and test equipment in the cockpit and cabin and perform a general aircraft inspection. They also check auxiliary power units (APUs) and engines. ETOPS-qualified mechanics perform additional checks for the engines as part of the ETOPS programme.
- Service check — mechanics from all disciplines perform in-depth checks of systems, including hydraulics, avionics and electrical systems, as well as additional time-controlled tasks. Inspectors check the insides of engines using fibre-optic cable or a borescope. Previous checks listed above are duplicated in greater detail.
- Letter check (A-check, B-check, C-check or D-check) — about 50 maintenance personnel from all disciplines participate. Delta's Tech Ops at Dallas/Fort Worth handle all 767-300ER letter checks. The aircraft is inspected by quality assurance personnel. Mechanics test engines, check and lubricate systems and repair cabin and cargo items. Aircraft (hangar) mechanics perform FAA-mandated modifications and repair any structural items. Letter checks are split into two visits at intervals of every 2,000 hours flight time or every six months. This approach allows Delta to avoid adding aircraft to the fleet to support a 24hr-a-day maintenance visit.
- Mid-visit — this in-depth inspection involves aircraft 'wet areas', such as the galleys, lavatories and bag bins. Aircraft (hangar) mechanics remove panels and conduct structural and corrosion checks throughout the aircraft. Previous checks are replicated in more detail.
- Heavy maintenance visit (HMV) — at an HMV aircraft (hangar) mechanics in overhaul bays perform the most in-depth of all the maintenance appraisals. Mechanics remove the seats, carpeting, floor and ceiling panels, disassemble cargo bays and open up all other panels to expose the aircraft's entire internal structure. Every system is removed and checked, involving all the maintenance specialists. Avionics components are removed from the aircraft and checked. Engines may be removed from the plane for overhaul by maintenance and propulsion engineering specialists. Fuel tanks are cleaned, inspected and repaired.

Right: *Delta's main maintenance hangar at its Technical Operations Center at Atlanta is one of the world's largest cantilevered buildings, being 1,600ft in length, 300ft wide and 93ft high.* Geoffrey P. Jones

The subsidiary shops that surround the main Maintenance Hangar at TOC are as follows:

- Engine Maintenance — over 700 engines per annum are repaired to support Delta and provide additional in-sourcing through the leasing of engines, APUs and landing gear. Personnel repair on average 13 engines every week. A complete engine overhaul depends on size, but can take between eight and 30 days and in Delta's unique engine maintenance system the complete work on one engine is ascribed to one crew throughout. Repairing and replacing parts accounts for approximately 65% of the cost of an engine repair. One set of the first stage turbine blades (48 pieces) used in the Pratt & Whitney 2037 engine (used in the Boeing 757) costs as much as $225,000.00. The list price for a Pratt & Whitney 4060 spare engine used in the Boeing 767-300ER, is more than $7 million.
- Thrust Reverser Shop — there are over 1,700 thrust reverser assemblies in use in Delta's current fleet, each with an average cost of $500,000. This shop maintains 60 rotatable spare thrust reverser units to support the whole fleet and is self-contained, with its own cleaning, percussion welding, painting and composite structural bonding capabilities. Other duties of this shop include repairing and modifying non-thrust reverser parts, such as engine throttle cables, actuators and fuel flow regulator boxes.
- Avionics Shops — the department for avionics at Atlanta has more than 250 mechanics and 39 team leaders. System-wide, all line mechanics at every Delta out-station are avionics qualified. These line mechanics are required to have 750hr of avionics training. Avionics installs, modifies, troubleshoots and repairs components that involve the following aircraft systems: navigation, fire detection/protection, communications, autopilot, entertainment, galley, lighting, fuel indicating and recording, traffic alert and collision avoidance system (TCAS) and windshear detection.
- Landing Gear Shop — overhauling a Lockheed L-1011 gear set (nose gear, port and starboard main gear) costs nearly $240,000, using $41,000 in materials and taking around 2,260 man-hours of work. Areas within the shop include assembly/disassembly, work-scope, machining repair, magnetic particle inspection, shot peen, oxide blasting, work control and material planning. Areas outside the main shop assist with the overhaul including engineering, plating and painting. Delta's landing gear shop is also now used by customers from other airlines.
- Wheel and Brake Shop — in an average year the 39 maintenance personnel in this shop process more than 19,000 wheels and 6,000 brakes. An aircraft brake weight ranges from 95lb (43kg) for the carbon Boeing 757 brake, to as much as 420lb (191kg) for the steel L-1011 brake. Service life of a tyre between changes ranges from 1.8 to 4 months depending on the aircraft type and number of landings per day. More tyre wear takes place during taxying than during a landing. The serviceable life of a brake between changes varies from 2.8 months for a Boeing 727 to 14 months for the 757.
- Sheet Metal Shop — this shop consists of the repair line, the flight control line, the manufacturing line and the drop-hammer shop. The repair line area is in charge of replacing acoustic panels on the nose cowl, with each panel costing $55,000, there are sometimes as many as four panels that may need replacing per cowl. The flight control line handles the leading edge slats, which are susceptible to damage in flight and on landing/take-off from hail and other foreign objects. The shop also replaces the trailing edge wedges at an average cost of $22,000 each, with eight to 10 slats per aircraft. The manufacturing line uses a 'trump' computer controlled machine which can cut a flat piece of metal into any shape imaginable. The older drop-hammer machine also manufactures parts for this shop. Staff from this shop have also been involved in the restoration and reskinning

of Delta's 'Ship 41' project of restoring to airworthy condition one of its original 1940 Douglas DC-3s (see separate chapter on the Delta Air Museum).

- Composite/Flap Shop — this shop repairs aircraft structures such as flaps, ailerons, rudders, engine nacelles, control surface trim tabs and radomes. In 1996 this shop repaired over 2,000 different parts. A new autoclave, used for composites, metal bonding and glass fibre work has been installed here at a cost of approximately $1.5 million. The autoclave 'cooks' repairs that require a positive pressure of up to 150psi (pounds per square inch) and temperatures exceeding 350° Fahrenheit. The composite team works with glass fibre, carbon fibre and other modern materials such as Kevlar. Composites are advanced materials, generally lighter and stronger than metals, and able more readily to resist pressure and high temperatures.
- Plasma Shop — this department sprays more than 40 different powders, used in engine part restoration. Four different thermo-spray processes are commonly used, plasma, power combustion, wire combustion and dual-wire. In these processes temperatures may exceed 30,000° Fahrenheit and noise levels may reach 130 decibels. This department has seven waterwash spray booths and state-of-the-art dust collection booths with gantry robotics were installed last year (1997). A waterstrip system is installed here, generating 55,000psi of water pressure and used to remove plasma coatings when parts arrive for rework.
- Paint Operations — this paint facility is huge and one of the newest and most modern in the world, able to accommodate a Boeing 747, L-1011 and Boeing 727 simultaneously. As well as its own aircraft, Delta's Atlanta paintshop has painted aircraft for Philippines Airlines, ATA, Air Jamaica, America West, VASP Brazil, Royal Jordanian, United Airlines (a Boeing 747), China Xinhua and corporate jets. Average time to strip and paint a narrowbody aircraft, such as a Boeing 727, is six days and a widebody, such as an MD-11, is 11 days. A narrowbody needs approximately 40 US gallons of paint (including primers) to repaint the exterior and a widebody approximately 80 US gallons. Each of the three paint bays has roof-mounted, remote-controlled stacker cranes or manned platforms which provide safe and easy access to the entire aircraft. They can position next to any area of the aircraft and have automatic sensors to prevent them hitting and damaging an aircraft. High-tech electrostatic spray equipment is used to paint aircraft. During the spraying process, the paint particles are electrically charged, and as a result are drawn to the surface of the aircraft. This process reduces the amount of paint particles that are released into the air or fall to the ground, saving paint and protecting the environment.

Third party aircraft maintenance is of growing importance as a source of income for Delta's TOC at Atlanta — in January 1998 the airline signed a contract valued at more than $130 million with Airborne Express and its fleet of up to 12 Boeing 767-200s. The contract commenced in April 1998 and runs until 2000 and involves engine services and other additional aircraft services. Airborne Express is the third largest express parcels carrier in the US.

Right: *A Heavy Maintenance Visit of an L-1011-500 TriStar at Delta's Atlanta TOC in April 1991.* Geoffrey P. Jones

Delta's Operations Control Center (OCC)

Opened in November 1995 within Delta Air Lines' corporate headquarters at Atlanta, the state-of-the-art Operations Control Center (OCC) is where the system-wide flight operations are controlled and monitored for 365 days a year and 24hr a day by a staff of 160 on duty at any one time. It was conceived and built between 1993 and 1995, partly as a result of severe weather disruption experienced during January 1993. It represents an investment by Delta of $450 million but is calculated to account for more than $35 million in savings per annum in respect of Irregular Flight Operations (IROPs). Delta will not let a problem with one aircraft disrupt its whole system.

OCC brings together in one place the airline's decision-makers in respect of gate-to-gate operations. It enables rapid communications, coupled with a focus on Delta's traveling customers, and has helped considerably in improving the travel experience for the quarter-million-plus passengers that Delta flies worldwide in any one day. It represents a proactive rather than a reactive approach to the management of the airline's operations.

An IROP will affect 3-10% of Delta's flights daily, usually as a result of weather problems, air traffic control restrictions, mechanical problems, medical emergencies or natural disasters. The main result of an IROP is the delay, diversion, misconnection or cancellation of a flight which impacts significantly on Delta's customers. With hub operations, where a passenger uses the hub as a cross-roads to connect with another onward flight — and these predominate in Delta's domestic US network — this is even more significant than if it were mainly a point-to-point carrier. Around 25% of the customer complaints that Delta receives relate to 'irregular operations', so the OCC is tasked with improving the travel experience of the airline's passengers.

OCC is like a NASA Spaceflight Mission Control facility. Dominating the front of the OCC are five huge video screens to give operational awareness and which carry broadcasts from the US's 24hr-a-day weather channel, real-time pictures surveying the ramps at the major Delta hubs — they could even display Frasier episodes if the Duty OCC allowed it!

There are 10 component sections to the OCC:

- the Bridge has the control positions for managers, representatives from the FAA's Air Traffic Control Services, marketing/ reservations, in-flight services and flight operations. They aid the quick, informed, integrated decision-making during critical IROPs situations.
- the Flight Superintendent dispatches flights, issues flight plans, is responsible for operational control, creates and implements irregular operations plans and is the co-ordination point for safe and efficient flight plan issue and tracking until completed.
- Meteorology prepares, issues and updates weather forecasts and advisories for the Flight Control Department, pilots and other Delta needs.
- System Re-Route section reviews and ensures flight crew availability for scheduled flights, reviewing and revising pilot and flight attendant rotations.
- Maintenance Control ensures the aircraft are airworthy.
- Equipment Control provides equipment coverage for Delta flights, works with maintenance co-ordinators and Flight Control to adjust aircraft routeing for maintenance and operational requirements.
- MEL Engineers are responsible for minimum equipment listing.
- Material Services ensure parts needed for maintenance activities are available.
- Navigation Database Analysts work closely with Flight Control and maintain the accuracy and integrity of the navigational database used to build flight plan routes.
- Radio section is responsible for air-to-ground radio communications concerning flight movements.

Delta believes its OCC is a world-leader in airline operations; this has only become possible due to present-day computer and communications technology. Flight planning is done from here for other airlines as well, including Aeroflot and CSA. OCC is primarily a customer-orientated facility, which in turn is cost motivated — to this end it also includes an analysis group that provides cost models and keeps daily tabs on what irregular operations are costing Delta. On the medical front the decision to place defibrillators and expanded emergency medical kits in each of the airline's 558 aircraft will both help passengers subject to medical emergencies and reduce the number of medically-driven flight diversions with their associated disruptions.

When you fly on Delta, 'Big Brother' is watching you closer than you think — from the OCC in Atlanta!

Left: *Delta's main Airport Control Center (ACC) perched high up on top of Alanta Worldport's Concourse 'A', where the Duty Chief Controller and his team co-ordinate all of Delta's ramp activity at the 80 gates it uses.* Geoffrey P. Jones

Below: *Opened in 1991, Delta's paint shop at its Atlanta Technical Operations Center (TOC) is one of the most modern in the world — it has three bays and can handle aircraft up to Boeing 747-400 size, but here a TriStar awaits a paint strip.* Geoffrey P. Jones

Delta's Air Museum

With a diverse history stretching back to 1924 and many hundreds of long-serving employees — one in New York has apparently worked for the airline for 65 years — there is a rich aviation legacy that Delta Air Lines has now formally recognised. Plans are well advanced for the establishment of a permanent Delta Air Lines museum at Atlanta Worldport at Hartsfield that will be open to the general public, probably next year (1999). The Delta Air Transport Heritage Museum, Inc has already been established.

The very first aircraft operated by Delta's predecessor was the Huff-Daland Duster. Fourteen of them were owned at one time or another between 1924 and 1929 when Dr B. R. (Bert) Coad and Collett Everman (C. E.) Woolman first experimented with powdered chemicals at Macon, Georgia and Monroe, Louisiana, using them in the world's first aerial crop-dusting operation in the battle against the deadly boll-weevil. Their means of application was the Huff-Daland Duster (Petrel 31), and one of these aircraft was restored in 1967 by Delta employees to a non-airworthy condition. It is permanently on loan to Delta from the National Air & Space Museum collection at the Smithsonian Institute in Washington, DC and is on display at Atlanta in the aircraft's original colours. During 1997 this Huff-Daland Duster was shipped north from Atlanta and suspended from the ceiling in the Terminal 3 building at Delta's Cincinnati/Northern Kentucky International Airport hub as part of the airport's 50th anniversary celebrations. It returned to Atlanta in July 1997, where it is likely to stay, unairworthy.

Below: *The original Huff-Daland Duster biplane used by Delta's predecessor in 1924 to start the world's first aerial crop-dusting operation, now hanging from the ceiling at the new Delta Air Museum in Atlanta.* Geoffrey P. Jones

After aerial crop-dusting, C. E.Woolman turned his attention to passengers. On 3 December 1928 Delta Air Service, Inc was formed. Early in 1929 they purchased the assets of Fox Flying Service, which included two Travel Air Model S-6000Bs, Delta's first passenger aircraft and operating under the name of Delta Air Service, Inc. In 1985 Delta acquired from Delta's Capt Doug Rounds a restored 1931 Curtiss-Wright Travel Air 6B Sedan, an aircraft that closely resembles Delta's original 1929 Travel Air. Although it wears the original tail-number NC8878 and colour scheme of Delta Air Service, it is only representative of a Travel Air S-6000B. Its last flight in the 1980s was on 15 September 1986 between Columbia (South Carolina) and Atlanta. Here a group of Delta employees completely restored the aircraft and it flew again in 1997. In September 1997 it was flown from Atlanta to Orlando for the first anniversary celebration on 30 September of Delta Express. The aircraft is kept in airworthy condition, its engine is run every week and, if weather conditions permit, makes brief circuits at Atlanta Worldport. When the museum is opened it will be prominently displayed in front of a replica façade of Delta Air Lines' original headquarters building located at Monroe, Louisiana.

Pride of place in the museum will go to 'Ship 41'. This is a DC-3 that is expected to fly again during 1998 after many years and was one of the original five DC-3s ordered by Delta Air Lines in 1940. Ship 41 NC28341, s/n 3278, was delivered to the airline on 23 December 1940 and was the first DC-3 used on commercial passenger services by Delta on 25 December. Delta used this aircraft for 18 years before it was sold to North Central Airlines. It was discovered, after much research by Delta retirees in 1990, derelict and in poor condition in Puerto Rico. The aircraft had flown with Air Puerto Rico as N29PR. Their idea was to obtain one of the airline's original DC-3s and restore it to airworthy condition. After about two years of negotiations, Delta acquired the remains of Ship 41 and brought it back to Atlanta in mid-1993. Since then a slow and pain-staking from-the-ground-up restoration has been in progress.

Some of the work has continued with retirees and other volunteers; there has been considerable corporate assistance and more recently, under the direction of James Ray, Manager of Delta's Museum Restoration Program, up to eight of Delta's full-time employees have been seconded to the Ship 41 restoration project to help complete it. The work during late winter/spring 1998 consisted of assembling all the component parts, many of which had been sub-contracted out, including to other Delta retirees. The whole fuselage has been rebuilt using parts cannibalised from two other DC-3s and newly manufactured components. New stringers, skins and a complete new cockpit area have been fabricated and assembled. Corporate help has come from a variety of sources throughout the US: ailerons from Delta's Tampa maintenance facility; radios donated by Collins, Inc; the fabric surfaces on the elevators from Fayetteville, Georgia; the engines and accessories from JRS Enterprises, Inc in Minnesota; brake assemblies, landing gear and hydraulic valves from Basler, Inc at Oshkosh, Wisconsin, and cowl flaps and oil cooler scoops from Vintage Aircraft, Inc at Collins, Colorado.

Ship 41 is to be painted in Delta's 1940s colours and operated under VFR (visual flight rules) in the 'private category', carrying non-fare-paying guests, touring the US promoting Delta Air Lines and visiting airshows and fly-ins.

A vast array of other historic Delta Air Lines artifacts are also under the jurisdiction of the Delta Heritage Museum — photos, uniforms, airport equipment, press cuttings, etc. For further information or if you have anything relating to Delta you would like to donate, contact James P. Ray at Dept. 914, PO Box 20585, Atlanta, GA 30320-2585, USA or telephone on +44 (1) 404 715 7883 or fax +44 (1) 404 715 2037.

Below: *In the final stages of assembly at Alanta in March 1998 after a complete refurbishment and restoration. Delta's Ship 41 was rescued from dereliction in Puerto Rico and is scheduled to fly again in Delta's 1940s colours in 1998.*
Geoffrey P. Jones

Boeing 737-200 (as used by Delta Express), other 737-200s, 737-300 and 737-347

	737-200 (DE)	*737-200*	*737-300*	*737-347*
First Flight of Boeing 737:	9 April 1967			
Wingspan:	93ft (28.35m)	93ft (28.35m)	94ft 9in (28.89m)	94ft 9in (28.89m)
Wing area:	1,098sq ft (102sq m)			
Length:	100ft 2in (30.53m)	100ft 2in (30.53m)	109ft 7in (33.41m)	109ft 7in (33.41m)
Height:	37ft (11.28m)	37ft (11.28m)	36ft 6in (11.13m)	36ft 6in (11.13m)
Cabin diameter:	12ft 4in (3.76m)	12ft 4in (3.76m)	12ft 4in (3.76m)	12ft 4in (3.76m)
Seating:	2 pilots 3 flt attendants 119 pax (one class)	2 pilots 4 flt attendants 107 pax (12F/95Y)	2 pilots 4 flt attendants 128 pax (8F/120Y)	2 pilots 4 flt attendants 128 pax (8F/120Y)
Cargo volume: (containerised):	875cu ft (24.78cu m)	850cu ft (24.07cu m)	1,068cu ft (30.25cu m)	1,068cu ft (30.25cu m)
Fuel capacity:	34,619lb (15,736kg) 5,167 USgal	34,619lb (15,736kg) 5,167 USgal	35,583lb (16,174kg) 5,311 USgal	35,583lb 5,311 USgal
Weight empty:	60,790lb (27,574kg)			
Max take-off weight:	115,500lb (52,500kg)	115,500lb	130,000lb (59,091kg)	130,000lb
Max landing weight:	103,000lb (46,818kg)	103,000lb	114,000lb (51,818kg)	114,000lb
Range (at full capacity):	1,400 statute miles	1,400 s. miles	1,600 s. miles	1,600 s. miles
Cruising speed:	426kt/490mph (810km/h)Mach 0.74	426kt/490mph (788km/h)Mach 0.73	435kt/500mph (788km/h)Mach 0.73	435kt/500mph (810km/h)Mach 0.74
Powerplant:	2 x Pratt & Whitney JT8D-15A	same	2 x GE CFM56-3-B1	same
Total thrust per engine:	31,000lb 12,400hp	31,000lb 12,400hp	40,000lb 16,000hp	40,000lb 16,000hp
Service ceiling:	37,000ft (11,280m)	same	same	same
Planes in service:	25	29	13	13

McDonnell Douglas MD-11

First flight of MD-11:	10 January 1990
Wingspan:	169ft 6in (51.6m)
Wing area:	3,648sq ft (338.9sq m)
Length:	200ft 10in (61.2m)
Height:	57ft 9in (17.6m)
Cabin diameter:	18ft 8in (5.7m)
Seating:	2 pilots 12 flight attendants 248 pax (18/33/197) — 11 aircraft; or 260 pax —three aircraft
Cargo vol (containerised):	5,278cu ft (150cu m)
Fuel capacity:	285,066lb (129,303kg) 42,547 USgal (161,057l)
Weight empty:	288,880lb (131,035kg)
Max take-off weight:	618,000lb (280,318kg)
Max landing weight:	430,000lb (195,048kg)
Range (at full capacity):	8,230 statute miles (13,244km)
Cruising speed:	478kt / 550mph (885km/h) Mach 0.82
Powerplant:	3 x Pratt & Whitney PW4460
Total thrust per engine:	60,000lb / 28,600hp
Service ceiling:	43,200ft (13,167m)
First delivery to Delta:	November 1990 with two leased aircraft

Above: *First of the 15 MD-11s in Delta's current fleet, N801DE lifts off from Alanta Worldport in March 1998. Note the wingtip winglets, one of the easy distinguishing features between the MD-11 and DC-10.* Geoffrey P. Jones

McDonnell Douglas MD-88 and MD-90

	MD-88	***MD-90***
First flight date:	15 August 1987	22 February 1993
Wingspan:	107ft 10in (32.87m)	107ft 10in (32.87m)
Wing area:	1,239sq ft (115.1sq m)	1,209sq ft (112.32sq m)
Length:	147ft 10in (45.06m)	152ft 7in (46.51m)
Height:	30ft 6in (9.3m)	30ft 6in (9.3m)
Cabin diameter:	11ft 0in (3.35m)	11ft 0in (3.35m)
Seating:	2 pilots 4 flight attendants 142 pax (14F/128Y)	2 pilots 4 flight attendants 150 pax (12F/138Y)
Cargo volume:	1,253cu ft (35.62cu m)	1,300cu ft (36.81cu m)
Fuel capacity:	39,128lb (17,748kg) 5,840 USgal	
Weight empty:	78,528lb (35,620kg)	88,000lb (39,916kg)
Max take-off weight:	149,500lb (67,812kg)	156,000lb (70,760kg)
Max landing weight:	130,000lb (58,967kg)	142,000lb (64,410kg)
Range (at full capacity):	1,490 statute miles	2,620 statute miles
Cruising speed:	454kt/522mph (846km/h) Mach 0.78	438kt/504mph (811k/mh) Mach 0.76
Powerplant:	2 x Pratt & Whitney JT8D-219	2 x Intn. Aero EngineV2525-D-5 turbofans
Total thrust per engine:	40,000lb 16,000hp	25,000lb 10,000hp
Service ceiling:	37,000ft (11,280m)	37,000ft (11,280m)
First delivery to Delta:	5 January 1988 (Delta was launch customer for the MD-88 and the MD-90)	February 1995
Planes in service:	120	11 (initial order for 31)

Boeing 727-200 and Boeing727-232

	B-727-200 'Advanced'	***B-727-232 'Long Range'***
First flight of Boeing 727:	9 February 1963	
Wingspan:	108ft 0in (33m)	108ft 0in (33m)
Wing area:	1,700sq ft (157.9sq m)	1,700sq ft (157.9sq m)
Length:	153ft 2in (46.7m)	153ft 2in (46.7m)
Height:	34ft (10.4m)	34ft (10.4m)
Cabin diameter:	12ft 4in (3.8m)	12ft 4in (3.8m)
Seating:	2 pilots/1 flight engineer 4 flight attendants 138 pax (8F/130Y)*	2 pilots/1 flight engineer 4 flight attendants 148 pax (12F/136Y)*
Cargo volume:	1,454cu ft (41cu m)	1,249cu ft (35.3cu m)
Fuel capacity:	54,200lb (24,585kg) 8,090 USgal	59,965lb (27,257kg) 8,950 USgal
Weight empty:	101,100lb (45,900kg)	101,100lb (45,900kg)
Max take-off weight:	184,000lb (83,462kg)	190,500lb (88,863kg)
Max landing weight:	154,500lb (70,081kg)	154,500lb (70,081kg)
Range (at full capacity):	1,515 statute miles	1,855 statute miles
Cruising speed:	460kt/529mph (851km/h) Mach 0.79	460kt/529mph (851km/h Mach 0.79)
Powerplant:	3 x P&W JT8D-15A	3 x P&W JT8D-15A
Total thrust per engine:	46,500lb 18,600hp	46,500lb 18,600hp
Service ceiling:	42,000ft (12,802m)	42,000ft (12,802m)
First delivery to Delta:	May 1972 when Northeast Airlines merged with Delta. Delta's own first 727 delivered January 1973.	
Planes in service:	115	14

*727-200 — 110 aircraft accommodate 149 passengers and five aircraft 120 passengers
727-232 — 12 aircraft accommodate 157 passengers and two aircraft 139 passengers

Boeing 757-232

First flight of Boeing 757:	19 February 1982
Wingspan:	124ft 6in (37.9m)
Wing area:	1,994sq ft (185.25sq m)
Length:	155ft 2in (47.4m)
Height:	44ft 6in (13.56m)
Cabin diameter:	12ft 4in (3.8m)
Seating:	2 pilots 6 flight attendants 183 pax (12F/171Y)*
Cargo volume:	1,785cu ft (50.5cu m)
Fuel capacity:	75,395lb (34,270kg)/ 11,253 USgal
Weight empty:	184,000lb (83,460kg)
Max take-off weight:	230,000lb (104,325kg)
Max landing weight:	198,000lb (89,810kg)
Range (at full capacity):	2,550 statute miles
Cruising speed:	459kt/528mph (850km/h) Mach 0.78
Powerplant:	2 x Pratt & Whitney PW2037
Total thrust per engine:	38,200lb / 15,280hp
Service ceiling:	42,000ft (12,810m)
First delivery to Delta:	28 November 1984 (service entry date — Delta was launch customer for the more powerful PW2037-powered version, placing an order for 60 on 12 Nov '80.
Planes in service:	91

*38 aircraft in Delta's 757-232 fleet accommodate 180 pax, four aircraft accommodate 182 pax and 49 aircraft accommodate 183 pax.

Above: *N616DL Boeing 757-232 a split-second before touchdown at Atlanta Worldport in March 1998.* Geoffrey P. Jones

Boeing 767-232, 767-332 and 767-332ER

	767-232	*767-332*	*767-332ER**
First flight of B-767:	26 September 1981		19 December 1986
Wingspan:	156ft 4in (47.6m)	156ft 4in (47.6m)	156ft 4in (47.6m)
Wing area:	3,050sq ft (283.2sq m)	3,050sq ft (283.2sq m)	3,050sq ft (283.2sq m)
Length:	159ft 2in (48.51m)	180ft 3in (54.94m)	180ft 3in (54.94m)
Height:	52ft (15.8m)	52ft (15.8m)	52ft (15.8m)
Cabin diameter:	16ft 6in (5m)	16ft 6in (5m)	16ft 6in (5m)
Seating:	2 pilots	2 pilots	2 pilots
	6 flight attendants	6 flight attendants	11 flt attendants
	204 pax (18F/186Y)	252 pax (24F/228Y)	212 pax (10F/28C/174Y)
Cargo volume: container	2,280cu ft (64.8cu m)	3,420cu ft (97.2cu m)	3,480cu ft (98.9cu m)**
Cargo volume: bulk	430cu ft (12cu m)	430cu ft (12cu m)	430cu ft (12cu m)
Fuel capacity:	111,890lb (50,859kg)	111,890lb (50,859kg)	161,740lb (73,365kg)
	16,700 USgal (63,126l)	16,700 USgal (63,126l)	24,140 USgal (91,380l)
Weight empty:	163,100lb (73,981kg)	173,700lb (78,789kg)	176,713lb (80,156kg)
Max take-off weight:	300,000lb (136,078kg)	345,000lb (156,489kg)	407,000lb (184,615kg)
Max landing weight:	270,000lb (122,470kg)	295,000lb (134,091kg)	320,000lb (145,152kg)
Range (at full capacity):	2,150 statute miles	2,600 statute miles	7,040 statute miles
Cruising speed:	461kt/530mph (858km/h)	461kt/530mph (858km/h)	471kt/542mph (872km/h)
	Mach 0.80	Mach 0.80	Mach 0.82
Powerplant:	2 x GE CF6-80A2	2 x GE CF6-80A2	2 x P&W PW4060
Total thrust per engine:	100,000lb/40,000hp	100,000lb/40,000hp	120,000lb/48,000hp
Service ceiling:	43,100ft (13,106m)	43,100ft (13,106m)	43,100ft (13,106m)
First delivery to Delta:	15 December 1982	November 1986	1990
Planes in service:	15	26	32

B-767-300ER — 26 aircraft accommodate 212 pax, three aircraft accommodate 203 pax and three aircraft accommodate 206 pax

** B-767-200 accommodates 22 x LD-2 containers and B-767-300 and 767-300ER 30 x LD-2 containers.

Lockheed L-1011-1, L-1011-250 and L-1011-500

	L-1011-1	*L-1011-250*	*L-1011-500*
First Flight of L-1011:	16 November 1970		
Wingspan:	155ft 4in (47.36m)	155ft 4in (47.36m)	164ft 4in (50.1m)
Length:	178ft 8in (54.7m)	178ft 8in (54.7m)	164ft 2in (50.05m)
Height:	55ft 4in (16.87m)	55ft 4in (16.87m)	55ft 4in (16.87m)
Cabin diameter:	19ft 7in (5.97m)	19ft 7in (5.97m)	19ft 7in (5.97m)
Seating:	2 pilots/1 flt eng	2 pilots/1 flt eng	2 pilots/1 flt eng*
	8 flight attendants	8 flight attendants	8 flight attendants
	302 pax (32F/270Y)	321 pax (30F/26C/265Y)	218 pax (12F/23C/183Y)
Cargo volume: container	3,084cu ft	2,384cu ft	3,266cu ft
Cargo volume: bulk	700cu ft	700cu ft	435cu ft
Fuel capacity:	159,560lb (72,527kg)	213,640lb (97,109kg)	213,640lb (97,109kg)
	23,814 USgal	31,887 USgal	31,887 USgal
Max take-off weight:	430,000lb (195,455kg)	510,000lb (231,818kg)	510,000lb (231,818kg)
Max landing weight:	348,000lb (158,182kg)	368,000lb (167,272kg)	368,000lb (167,272kg)
Range (at full capacity):	3,670 statute miles	5,700 statute miles	5,505 statute miles
Range (limited payload):	2,800 statute miles	5,000 statute miles	5,195 statute miles
Cruising speed:	480kt/552mph (894km/h)	477kt/548mph (888km/h)	477kt/548mph (888km/h)
	Mach 0.83	Mach 0.82	Mach 0.82
Powerplant:	3 x R-R RB.211-22B	3 x R-R RB.211-524B4	3 x R-R RB.211-524B4
Total thrust per engine:	126,000lb	150,000lb	150,000lb
	62,000hp	69,000hp	69,000hp
Service ceiling:	42,000ft (12,805m)	42,000ft (12,805m)	43,000ft (13,110m)
First delivery to Delta:	25 December 1973	15 April 1978	13 May 1979
Planes in service:	23	6	17

*L-1011-500 — nine aircraft accommodate 218 pax, five aircraft accommodate 243 pax, two aircraft accommodate 249 pax and one aircraft accommodates 241 pax.

Boeing 777-200IGW (Increased Gross Weight)

First flight of B777:	12 June 1994 (26 May 1995 for Rolls-Royce-powered B-777)
Wingspan:	199ft 11in (60.93m)
Wing area:	4,605sq ft (427.82sq m)
Length:	209ft 1in (63.73m)
Height:	60ft 9in (18.52m)
Cabin diameter:	19ft 3in (5.87m)
Seating:	2 pilots 12 flight attendants 292 pax (12F/46B/234Y)
Cargo volume: container	5,656cu ft (160.16cu m) in 32 LD-3 containers 600cu ft (16.99cu m) of bulk cargo
Fuel capacity:	299,490lb (136,132kg) 44,700 USgal
Weight empty:	304,790lb (138,250kg) operating long-range
Max take-off weight:	648,000lb (294,545kg)
Max landing weight:	460,000lb (209,091kg)
Range (at full capacity):	6,905-7,535 statute miles
Cruising speed:	490kt/564mph (913km/h) Mach 0.84
Powerplant:	2 x R-R Trent 892
Total thrust per engine:	92,000lb/46,000hp
Sevice ceiling:	43,000ft (13,100m)
First delivery to Delta:	Scheduled for August 1999 to December 2000
Planes in service:	None — 10 on order with 20 options

Aircraft of Delta's Affiliated Commuter Airlines (Delta Connection)

Canadair (Bombardier) CRJ.100

Airlines:	ASA/Comair/SkyWest	Length:	87ft 10in (26.77m)	Cruising speed:	424kt/488mph (768km/h) Mach 0.74
First flight date:	10 May 1991	Height:	19ft 3in (5.87m)	Powerplant:	2 x GE CF34-3A1 turbofans
Wingspan:	69ft 7in (21.21m)	Seating:	2 pilots/50 pax		
		Range:	1,128 statute miles		

Embraer EMB-120 Brasilia

Airlines:	ASA/Comair/SkyWest/TransStates	Length:	65ft 8in (20m)	Cruising speed:	264kt/304mph (552km/h)
First flight date:	27 July 1983	Height:	20ft 10in (6.35m)	Powerplant:	2 x P&W Canada PW18 turboprops
Wingspan:	64ft 11in (19.78m)	Seating:	2 pilots/30 pax		
		Range:	920 statute miles		

Saab 340 and 340B

Airline:	BEX	Length:	64ft 9in (19.73m)	Cruising speed:	424kt/488mph (768km/h) Mach 0.74
First flight date:	25 January 1983 (SF340)	Height:	22ft 6.5in (6.87m)	Powerplant:	2 x GE CT7-9B turboprops
Wingspan:	70ft 4in (21.44m)	Seating:	2 pilots/33-5 pax		
		Range:	927 (A) and 1,076 (B) statute miles		

AI(R) ATR-42

Airline:	TransStates	Length:	74ft 4in (22.67m)	Powerplant:	2 x P&W Canada PW120 turboprops
First flight date:	August 1984	Height:	24ft 10in (7.59m)		
Wingspan:	80ft 7in (24.57m)	Seating:	2 pilots/50 pax		
		Range:	617 statute miles		

AI(R) ATR-72

Airline:	ASA/TransStates	Length:	89ft 2in (27.17m)	Powerplant:	2 x P&W Canada PW124B turboprops
First flight date:	October 1984	Height:	25ft 1in (7.65m)		
Wingspan:	88ft 9in (27.05m)	Seating:	2 pilots/74 pax		
		Range:	531 statute miles		

BAe/AI(R) Jetstream 32 and Jetstream 41

	Jetstream 32	*Jetstream 41*
Airline:	TransStates	TransStates
First flight date:	March 1980	September 1991
Wingspan:	52ft (15.85m)	60ft 5in (18.42m)
Length:	47ft 2in (14.37m)	63ft 2in (19.25m)
Height:	17ft 8in (5.38m)	18ft 10in (5.74m)
Seating:	2 pilots/ 19 pax	2 pilots/ 29 pax
Range:	796 statute miles	796 statute miles
Powerplant:	2 x Allied Signal TPE331.14 t'props	2 x Allied Signal TPE331.14 t'props

Delta Air Lines Fleet List

Boeing 727-200 Series

Regn	*Aircraft Type*	*Fleet No*	*Notes/Name*
N282WA	Boeing 727-247	579	All registrations suffixed WA are ex-Western Airlines
N283WA	Boeing 727-247	580	
N290WA	Boeing 727-247	582	
N291WA	Boeing 727-247	583	
N292WA	Boeing 727-247	584	
N293WA	Boeing 727-247	585	
N294WA	Boeing 727-247	586	
N295WA	Boeing 727-247	587	
N296WA	Boeing 727-247	588	
N297WA	Boeing 727-247	589	
N400DA	Boeing 727-232	400	
N401DA	Boeing 727-232	401	
N402DA	Boeing 727-232	402	
N403DA	Boeing 727-232	403	
N404DA	Boeing 727-232	404	
N405DA	Boeing 727-232	405	
N406DA	Boeing 727-232	406	
N407DA	Boeing 727-232	407	
N408DA	Boeing 727-232	408	
N409DA	Boeing 727-232	409	
N410DA	Boeing 727-232	410	
N411DA	Boeing 727-232	411	
N412DA	Boeing 727-232	412	Delta Shuttle aircraft
N413DA	Boeing 727-232	413	Delta Shuttle aircraft
N414DA	Boeing 727-232	414	Delta Shuttle aircraft
N415DA	Boeing 727-232	415	Delta Shuttle aircraft
N416DA	Boeing 727-232	416	
N417DA	Boeing 727-232	417	Delta Shuttle aircraft
N418DA	Boeing 727-232	418	
N419DA	Boeing 727-232	419	
N420DA	Boeing 727-232	420	
N421DA	Boeing 727-232	421	
N466DA	Boeing 727-232	466	
N467DA	Boeing 727-232	467	
N468DA	Boeing 727-232	468	
N469DA	Boeing 727-232	469	
N470DA	Boeing 727-232	470	
N471DA	Boeing 727-232	471	
N472DA	Boeing 727-232	472	Delta Shuttle aircraft
N474DA	Boeing 727-232	474	Delta Shuttle aircraft
N475DA	Boeing 727-232	475	
N476DA	Boeing 727-232	476	
N477DA	Boeing 727-232	477	
N478DA	Boeing 727-232	478	
N479DA	Boeing 727-232	479	Delta Shuttle aircraft
N480DA	Boeing 727-232	480	Delta Shuttle aircraft
N481DA	Boeing 727-232	481	Delta Shuttle aircraft
N482DA	Boeing 727-232	482	
N483DA	Boeing 727-232	483	
N484DA	Boeing 727-232	484	
N485DA	Boeing 727-232	485	

Above: *Hangared for maintainance at Delta's TOC at Atlanta in April 1991, Boeing 727-232 N494DA, Fleet No 494, with two of the airline's Boeing 757-232s beyond.* Geoffrey P. Jones

Regn	Aircraft Type	Fleet No	Notes/Name
N489DA	Boeing 727-232	489	
N490DA	Boeing 727-232	490	
N491DA	Boeing 727-232	491	Delta Shuttle aircraft
N492DA	Boeing 727-232	492	
N493DA	Boeing 727-232	493	
N494DA	Boeing 727-232	494	
N495DA	Boeing 727-232	495	
N496DA	Boeing727-232	496	
N497DA	Boeing 727-232	497	
N498DA	Boeing 727-232	498	
N499DA	Boeing 727-232	499	
N501DA	Boeing 727-232	501	
N502DA	Boeing 727-232	502	
N503DA	Boeing 727-232	503	
N504DA	Boeing 727-232	504	
N505DA	Boeing 727-232	505	
N506DA	Boeing 727-232	506	
N507DA	Boeing 727-232	507	
N508DA	Boeing 727-232	508	
N509DA	Boeing 727-232	509	
N510DA	Boeing 727-232	510	
N511DA	Boeing 727-232	511	Valsan winglets fitted
N512DA	Boeing 727-232	512	
N513DA	Boeing 727-232	513	
N514DA	Boeing 727-232	514	
N515DA	Boeing 727-232	515	
N516DA	Boeing 727-232	516	
N517DA	Boeing 727-232	517	
N518DA	Boeing 727-232	518	
N519DA	Boeing 727-232	519	
N520DA	Boeing 727-232	520	
N521DA	Boeing 727-232	521	
N522DA	Boeing 727-232	522	
N523DA	Boeing 727-232	523	
N524DA	Boeing 727-232	524	
N525DA	Boeing 727-232	525	
N526DA	Boeing 727-232	526	
N527DA	Boeing 727-232	527	
N528DA	Boeing 727-232	528	
N529DA	Boeing 727-232	529	
N531DA	Boeing 727-232	531	
N532DA	Boeing 727-232	532	
N533DA	Boeing 727-232	533	
N534DA	Boeing 727-232	534	
N535DA	Boeing 727-232	535	
N536DA	Boeing 727-232	536	
N537DA	Boeing 727-232	537	
N538DA	Boeing 727-232	538	ex-N1786B
N539DA	Boeing 727-232	539	
N540DA	Boeing 727-232	540	
N541DA	Boeing 727-232	541	
N542DA	Boeing 727-232	542	
N543DA	Boeing 727-232	543	
N544DA	Boeing 727-232	544	
N545DA	Boeing 727-232	545	
N546DA	Boeing 727-232	546	

Above: *Taxying out in front of Concourse 'B' at Atlanta Worldport in March 1998 is Boeing 727-232 N475DA.*
Geoffrey P. Jones

Regn	Aircraft Type	Fleet No	Notes/Name
N805EA	Boeing 727-225	590	purchased from CIT Group Sep 1997
N830WA	Boeing 727-247	577	
N831L	Boeing 727-2Q8	581	
N831WA	Boeing 727-247	578	
N2807W	Boeing 727-247	557	
N2809W	Boeing 727-247	559	
N2810W	Boeing 727-247	560	
N2811W	Boeing 727-247	561	
N2812W	Boeing 727-247	562	
N2813W	Boeing 727-247	563	
N2814W	Boeing 727-247	564	
N2815W	Boeing 727-247	565	
N2816W	Boeing 727-247	566	
N2817W	Boeing 727-247	567	
N2819W	Boeing 727-247	568	
N2820W	Boeing 727-247	569	
N2821W	Boeing 727-247	570	
N2829W	Boeing 727-247	576	
N8873Z	Boeing 727-225	445	
N8875Z	Boeing 727-225	441	
N8882Z	Boeing 727-225	591	purchased from Residco, Aug 1997 (ex-Kiwi Intl A/L)
N8889Z	Boeing 727-225	440	
N8890Z	Boeing 727-225	438	
N8891Z	Boeing 727-225	439	

Boeing 727 fleet total — 131 aircraft

Boeing 737-200 Series

Regn	Aircraft Type	Fleet No	Notes/Name
N235WA	Boeing 737-2J8	359	ex-N4562N
N236WA	Boeing 737-247	360	
N237WA	Boeing 737-247	361	
N238WA	Boeing 737-247	362	
N239WA	Boeing 737-247	363	
N242WA	Boeing 737-247	364	
N243WA	Boeing 737-247	365	
N244WA	Boeing 737-247	366	
N245WA	Boeing 737-247	372	
N301DL	Boeing 737-232	301	Delta Express
N302DL	Boeing 737-232	302	Delta Express
N303DL	Boeing 737-232	303	Delta Express
N304DL	Boeing 737-232	304	Delta Express
N305DL	Boeing 737-232	305	Delta Express
N306DL	Boeing 737-232	306	Delta Express
N307DL	Boeing 737-232	307	Delta Express
N308DL	Boeing 737-232	308	Delta Express
N309DL	Boeing 737-232	309	Delta Express
N310DA	Boeing 737-232	310	Delta Express
N311DL	Boeing 737-232	311	Delta Express
N312DL	Boeing 737-232	312	Delta Express
N313DL	Boeing 737-232	313	Delta Express
N314DL	Boeing 737-232	314	Delta Express
N315DL	Boeing 737-232	315	Delta Express
N316DL	Boeing 737-232	316	Delta Express
N317DL	Boeing 737-232	317	Delta Express
N318DL	Boeing 737-232	318	Delta Express

Regn	*Aircraft Type*	*Fleet No*	*Notes/Name*
N319DL	Boeing 737-232	319	Delta Express
N320DL	Boeing 737-232	320	Delta Express
N321DL	Boeing 737-232	321	Delta Express
N322DL	Boeing 737-232	322	Delta Express
N323DL	Boeing 737-232	323	Delta Express
N324DL	Boeing 737-232	324	Delta Express
N325DL	Boeing 737-232	325	Delta Express
N326DL	Boeing 737-232	326	
N327DL	Boeing 737-232	327	
N328DL	Boeing 737-232	328	
N329DL	Boeing 737-232	329	
N330DL	Boeing 737-232	330	
N331DL	Boeing 737-232	331	
N332DL	Boeing 737-232	332	
N334DL	Boeing 737-232	333	
N367DL	Boeing 737-2S3	367	ex-EI-BPY
N369DL	Boeing 737-2S3	369	ex-N368DL
N373DL	Boeing 737-247	370	ex-N246WA
N374DL	Boeing 737-247	374	ex-N247WA
N375DL	Boeing 737-247	375	ex-N248WA
N376DL	Boeing 737-247	376	ex-N249WA
N377DL	Boeing 737-247	377	ex-N254WA
N378DL	Boeing 737-247	378	ex-N255WA
N379DL	Boeing 737-247	379	ex-N256WA
N380DL	Boeing 737-247	380	ex-N257WA
N381DL	Boeing 737-247	381	ex-N258WA
N382DL	Boeing 737-247	382	ex-N259WA

Boeing 737-200 fleet total — 54 aircraft

Boeing 737-300 Series

Regn	*Aircraft Type*	*Fleet No*	*Notes/Name*
N302WA	Boeing 737-347	202	Wally Bird
N303WA	Boeing 737-347	203	Salt Lake City
N304WA	Boeing 737-347	204	
N305WA	Boeing 737-347	205	
N306WA	Boeing 737-347	206	
N307WA	Boeing 737-347	207	
N308WA	Boeing 737-347	208	
N309WA	Boeing 737-347	209	
N311WA	Boeing 737-347	211	
N312WA	Boeing 737-347	212	
N313WA	Boeing 737-347	213	
N2310	Boeing 737-347	210	
N3301	Boeing 737-347	201	Larry Lee
N221DL	Boeing 737-35B		ex-D-AGEA purchased from Germania, Feb 1998
N222DZ	Boeing 737-35B		ex-D-AGEB
N223DZ	Boeing 737-35D		ex-D-AGEC
N224DA	Boeing 737-35B		ex-D-AGED
N225DL	Boeing 737-3L9		ex-D-AGEF
N231DN	Boeing 737-3L9		ex-D-AGEH
N232DZ	Boeing 737-3L9		ex-D-AGEI
N241DL	Boeing 737-330		ex-D-ABWA
N242DL	Boeing 737-330		ex-D-ABWB

Boeing 737-300 fleet total — 22 aircraft

Boeing 737-800 Series

Regn	*Aircraft Type*	*Notes/Name*
N371DA	Boeing 737-832	on order
N372DA	Boeing 737-832	on order
N373DA	Boeing 737-832	on order
N374DA	Boeing 737-832	on order
N375DA	Boeing 737-832	on order
N376DA	Boeing 737-832	on order
N377DA	Boeing 737-832	on order
N378DA	Boeing 737-832	on order
N379DA	Boeing 737-832	on order
N380DA	Boeing 737-832	on order
N381DA	Boeing 737-832	on order

A total of 70 Boeing 737-632/732/832s are on order for delivery between August 1998 and 2006.

Boeing 757-200 Series

Regn	*Aircraft Type*	*Fleet No*	*Notes/Name*
N601DL	Boeing 757-232	601	
N602DL	Boeing 757-232	602	
N603DL	Boeing 757-232	603	
N604DL	Boeing 757-232	604	
N605DL	Boeing 757-232	605	
N606DL	Boeing 757-232	606	
N607DL	Boeing 757-232	607	
N608DL	Boeing 757-232	608	
N609DL	Boeing 757-232	609	
N610DL	Boeing 757-232	610	
N611DL	Boeing 757-232	611	
N612DL	Boeing 757-232	612	
N613DL	Boeing 757-232	613	
N614DL	Boeing 757-232	614	
N615DL	Boeing 757-232	615	
N616DL	Boeing 757-232	616	
N617DL	Boeing 757-232	617	
N618DL	Boeing 757-232	618	
N619DL	Boeing 757-232	619	
N620DL	Boeing 757-232	620	
N621DL	Boeing 757-232	621	
N622DL	Boeing 757-232	622	
N623DL	Boeing 757-232	623	
N624DL	Boeing 757-232	624	
N625DL	Boeing 757-232	625	
N626DL	Boeing 757-232	626	
N627DL	Boeing 757-232	627	
N628DL	Boeing 757-232	628	
N629DL	Boeing 757-232	629	
N630DL	Boeing 757-232	630	
N631DL	Boeing 757-232	631	
N632DL	Boeing 757-232	632	
N633DL	Boeing 757-232	633	
N634DL	Boeing 757-232	634	
N635DL	Boeing 757-232	635	
N636DL	Boeing 757-232	636	
N637DL	Boeing 757-232	637	
N638DL	Boeing 757-232	638	
N639DL	Boeing 757-232	639	

Above: *N643DL Boeing 757-232, one of 91 currently in the Delta fleet in early 1998, seen here taxying for take-off at San Francisco International in June 1990.* Geoffrey P. Jones

Regn	*Aircraft Type*	*Fleet No*	*Notes/Name*
N640DL	Boeing 757-232	640	
N641DL	Boeing 757-232	641	
N642DL	Boeing 757-232	642	
N643DL	Boeing 757-232	643	
N644DL	Boeing 757-232	644	
N645DL	Boeing 757-232	645	
N646DL	Boeing 757-232	646	
N647DL	Boeing 757-232	647	
N648DL	Boeing 757-232	648	
N649DL	Boeing 757-232	649	
N650DL	Boeing 757-232	650	
N651DL	Boeing 757-232	651	
N652DL	Boeing 757-232	652	
N653DL	Boeing 757-232	653	
N654DL	Boeing 757-232	654	

Above: *The Boeing 757 first entered service with Delta Air Lines in February 1985 as a Boeing 727 replacement. N610DL is seen here on finals to land at Miami in April 1989.* Geoffrey P. Jones

N655DL	Boeing 757-232	655	
N656DL	Boeing 757-232	656	
N657DL	Boeing 757-232	657	
N658DL	Boeing 757-232	658	
N659DL	Boeing 757-232	659	
N660DL	Boeing 757-232	660	
N661DN	Boeing 757-232	661	
N662DN	Boeing 757-232	662	
N663DN	Boeing 757-232	663	
N664DN	Boeing 757-232	664	
N665DN	Boeing 757-232	665	
N666DN	Boeing 757-232	666	

Regn	Aircraft Type	Fleet No	Notes/Name
N667DN	Boeing 757-232	667	
N668DN	Boeing 757-232	668	
N669DN	Boeing 757-232	669	
N670DN	Boeing 757-232	670	
N671DN	Boeing 757-232	671	
N672DL	Boeing 757-232	672	
N673DL	Boeing 757-232	673	
N674DL	Boeing 757-232	674	
N675DL	Boeing 757-232	675	
N676DL	Boeing 757-232	676	
N677DL	Boeing 757-232	677	
N678DL	Boeing 757-232	678	
N679DA	Boeing 757-232	679	
N680DA	Boeing 757-232	680	
N681DA	Boeing 757-232	681	
N682DA	Boeing 757-232	682	
N683DA	Boeing 757-232	683	
N684DA	Boeing 757-232	684	
N685DA	Boeing 757-232	685	
N686DA	Boeing 757-232	686	
N687DL	Boeing 757-232	687	
N688DL	Boeing 757-232	688	
N689DL	Boeing 757-232	689	
N690DL	Boeing 757-232	690	
N692DA	Boeing 757-232	692	on order
N693DA	Boeing 757-232	693	on order
N694DA	Boeing 757-232	694	on order
N695DA	Boeing 757-232	695	on order
N696DA	Boeing 757-232	696	on order
N750AT	Boeing 757-212ER	6902	ex-9V-SGL
N751AT	Boeing 757-212ER	6901	ex-9V-SGK
N752AT	Boeing 757-212ER	6904	ex 9V-SGN
N753AT	Boeing 757-212ER		
N757AT	Boeing 757-212	6903	
N900PC	Boeing 757-232	691	leased from 757 Aircraft Investors in 1997

Boeing 757-200 Series total aircraft — 101aircraft

Boeing 767-200 Series

Regn	Aircraft Type	Fleet No	Notes/Name
N101DA	Boeing 767-232	101	
N102DA	Boeing 767-232	102	Spirit of Delta
N103DA	Boeing 767-232	103	
N104DA	Boeing 767-232	104	
N105DA	Boeing 767-232	105	
N106DA	Boeing 767-232	106	
N107DL	Boeing 767-232	107	
N108DL	Boeing 767-232	108	
N109DL	Boeing 767-232	109	
N110DL	Boeing 767-232	110	
N111DN	Boeing 767-232	111	
N112DL	Boeing 767-232	112	
N113DA	Boeing 767-232	113	
N114DL	Boeing 767-232	114	
N115DA	Boeing 767-232	115	

Boeing 767-200 series total — 15 aircraft

Boeing 767-300 Series

Regn	Aircraft Type	Fleet No	Notes/Name
N116DL	Boeing 767-332	116	
N117DL	Boeing 767-332	117	
N118DL	Boeing 767-332	118	
N119DL	Boeing 767-332	119	
N120DL	Boeing 767-332	120	
N121DE	Boeing 767-332	121	
N122DL	Boeing 767-332	122	
N123DN	Boeing 767-332	123	
N124DE	Boeing 767-332	124	
N125DL	Boeing 767-332	125	
N126DL	Boeing 767-332	126	
N127DL	Boeing 767-332	127	
N128DL	Boeing 767-332	128	
N129DL	Boeing 767-332	129	
N130DL	Boeing 767-332	130	
N131DN	Boeing 767-332	131	
N132DN	Boeing 767-332	132	
N133DN	Boeing 767-332	133	
N134DL	Boeing 767-332	134	
N135DL	Boeing 767-332	135	
N136DL	Boeing 767-332	136	
N137DL	Boeing 767-332	137	
N138DL	Boeing 767-332	138	
N139DL	Boeing 767-332	139	
N140LL	Boeing 767-332	1401	
N1402A	Boeing 767-332	1402	
N143DA	Boeing 767-332	143	
N144DA	Boeing 767-332	144	
N1501P	Boeing 767-3P6ER ex-A40-GL	1501	
N152DL	Boeing 767-3P6ER ex-A40-GM	1502	
N153DL	Boeing 767-3P6ER ex-A40-GN	1503	
N154DL	Boeing 767-3P6ER ex-A40-GO	1504	
N155DL	Boeing 767-3P6ER ex-A40-GP	1505	
N156DL	Boeing 767-3P6ER ex-A40-GR	1506	
N169DZ	Boeing 767-332ER		on order
N171DN	Boeing 767-332ER	171	
N171DZ	Boeing 767-332		on order
N172DN	Boeing 767-332ER	172	
N172DZ	Boeing 767-332		on order
N173DN	Boeing 767-332ER	173	
N173DZ	Boeing 767-332		on order
N174DN	Boeing 767-332ER	174	
N174DZ	Boeing 767-332		on order
N175DN	Boeing 767-332ER	175	
N175DZ	Boeing 767-332		on order
N176DN	Boeing 767-332ER	176	
N176DZ	Boeing 767-332		on order
N177DN	Boeing 767-332ER	177	
N177DZ	Boeing 767-332		on order
N178DN	Boeing 767-332ER	178	
N178DZ	Boeing 767-332		on order
N179DN	Boeing 767-332ER	179	
N179DZ	Boeing 767-332		on order
N180DN	Boeing 767-332ER	180	
N181DN	Boeing 767-332ER	181	

Left: *On push-back from one of the gates at Atlanta Worldport's Concourse 'A' in March 1998, Delta's Boeing 767-332 N129DL.*
Geoffrey P. Jones

Right: *The third Boeing 767-232 to join Delta's fleet in 1983 was N103DA, one of the smaller 200 series aircraft of which the airline has 15. This one is seen on turnaround at Atlanta in April 1991.*
Geoffrey P. Jones

Regn	*Aircraft Type*	*Fleet No*	*Notes/Name*
N182DN	Boeing 767-332ER	182	
N183DN	Boeing 767-332ER	183	
N184DN	Boeing 767-332ER	184	
N185DN	Boeing 767-332ER	185	
N186DN	Boeing 767-332ER	186	
N187DN	Boeing 767-332ER	187	
N188DN	Boeing 767-332ER	188	
N189DN	Boeing 767-332ER	189	
N190DN	Boeing 767-332ER	190	first aircraft in Delta's new colours, April '97
N191DN	Boeing 767-332ER	191	
N192DN	Boeing 767-332ER	192	
N193DN	Boeing 767-332	193	
N194DN	Boeing 767-332	194	
N195DN	Boeing 767-332	195	
N196DN	Boeing 767-332	196	
N197DN	Boeing 767-332	197	
N198DN	Boeing 767-332ER	198	Delivered February 1998
N199DN	Boeing 767-332ER	199	Delivered March 1998
N1200K	Boeing 767-332		on order
N1201P	Boeing 767-332		on order
N1402A	Boeing 767-332		on order

Boeing 767-300 Series total — 75 aircraft

Lockheed L-1011 TriStar Srs 100/200

Regn	*Aircraft Type*	*Fleet No*	*Notes/Name*
N714DA	Lockheed L-1011-1 TriStar	714	
N715DA	Lockheed L-1011-1 TriStar	715	now withdrawn from service
N716DA	Lockheed L-1011-1 TriStar	716	now withdrawn from service
N718DA	Lockheed L-1011-1 TriStar	718	
N719DA	Lockheed L-1011-1 TriStar	719	
N720DA	Lockheed L-1011-1 TriStar	720	
N721DA	Lockheed L-1011-1 TriStar	721	
N722DA	Lockheed L-1011-1 TriStar	722	
N723DA	Lockheed L-1011-1 TriStar	723	
N724DA	Lockheed L-1011-200 TriStar	724	withdrawn from service
N725DA	Lockheed L-1011-1 TriStar	725	
N727DA	Lockheed L-1011-1 TriStar	727	
N728DA	Lockheed L-1011-1 TriStar	728	
N729DA	Lockheed L-1011-1 TriStar	729	
N730DA	Lockheed L-1011-1 TriStar	730	

Regn	Aircraft Type	Fleet No	Notes/Name
N733DS	Lockheed L-1011-1 TriStar	733	
N735D	Lockheed L-1011-1 TriStar	735	
N736DY	Lockheed L-1011-250 TriStar	736	
N737D	Lockheed L-1011-250 TriStar	737	
N740DA	Lockheed L-1011-250 TriStar	740	
N741DA	Lockheed L-1011-250 TriStar	741	
N783DL	Lockheed L-1011-1 TriStar	783	ex-N305EA now withdrawn from service
N784DL	Lockheed L-1011-1 TriStar	784	ex-N317EA
N786DL	Lockheed L-1011-1 TriStar	786	ex-N332EA
N789DL	Lockheed L-1011-1 TriStar	789	ex-N335EA
N790DL	Lockheed L-1011-1 TriStar	790	ex-N336EA
N1731D	Lockheed L-1011-1 TriStar	731	
N1732D	Lockheed L-1011-1 TriStar	732	
N1734D	Lockheed L-1011-1 TriStar	734	
N1738D	Lockheed L-1011-250 TriStar	738	
N1739D	Lockheed L-1011-250 TriStar	739	

Lockheed L-1011-100/200 Series total — 31 aircraft

Left: *Ex-PanAm L-1011-500 TriStar N504PA, now N754DL with Delta, climbs away from Atlanta Worldport's runway 27L in March 1998, one of eight ex-PanAm TriStars in the fleet.* Geoffrey P. Jones

Lockheed L-1011 TriStar Srs 500

Regn	Aircraft Type	Fleet No	Notes/Name
N751DA	Lockheed L-1011-500 TriStar	751	now withdrawn from service
N752DA	Lockheed L-1011-500 TriStar	752	
N753DA	Lockheed L-1011-500 TriStar	753	
N754DL	Lockheed L-1011-500 TriStar	754	ex-N504PA
N755DL	Lockheed L-1011-500 TriStar	755	ex-N505PA
N756DR	Lockheed L-1011-500 TriStar	756	ex-N5507PA
N759DA	Lockheed L-1011-500 TriStar	759	ex-N501PA
N760DH	Lockheed L-1011-500 TriStar	760	ex-N510PA
N761DA	Lockheed L-1011-500 TriStar	761	ex-N513PA
N762DA	Lockheed L-1011-500 TriStar	762	ex-N514PA
N763DL	Lockheed L-1011-500 TriStar	763	ex-N512PA
N764DA	Lockheed L-1011-500 TriStar	764	ex-C-GAGF
N765DA	Lockheed L-1011-500 TriStar	765	ex-C-GAGG
N766DA	Lockheed L-1011-500 TriStar	766	ex-C-GAGH
N767DA	Lockheed L-1011-500 TriStar	767	ex-C-GAGI
N768DL	Lockheed L-1011-500 TriStar	768	ex-C-GAGJ
N769DL	Lockheed L-1011-500 TriStar	769	ex-C-GAGK

Lockheed L-1011-500 TriStar total — 17 aircraft

Above: *First of the Delta MD-11 fleet to wear the new livery, N802DE rotates at take-off.* Geoffrey P. Jones

McDonnell Douglas MD-11

Regn	Aircraft Type	Fleet No	Notes/Name
N801DE	MD-11	801	
N802DE	MD-11	802	
N803DE	MD-11	803	ex-N30075
N804DE	MD-11	804	
N805DE	MD-11	805	
N806DE	MD-11	806	
N807DE	MD-11	807	
N808DE	MD-11	808	
N809DE	MD-11	809	
N810DE	MD-11	810	
N811DE	MD-11	811	
N812DE	MD-11		Centennial Spirit ex-N6202S
N813DE	MD-11		ex-N90178
N814DE	MD-11		Delivered 20 Feb 1998
N815DE	MD-11		

McDonnell Douglas MD-11 total — 15 aircraft

McDonnell Douglas (Boeing) MD-88

Regn	Aircraft Type	Fleet No
N900DE	MD-88	9000
N901DE	MD-88	9001
N901DL	MD-88	901
N902DE	MD-88	9002
N902DL	MD-88	902
N903DE	MD-88	9003
N903DL	MD-88	903
N904DE	MD-88	9004
N904DL	MD-88	904
N905DE	MD-88	9005
N905DL	MD-88	905
N906DE	MD-88	9006
N906DL	MD-88	906
N907DE	MD-88	9007
N907DL	MD-88	907
N908DE	MD-88	9008
N908DL	MD-88	908

Regn	Aircraft Type	Fleet No
N909DE	MD-88	9009
N909DL	MD-88	909
N910DE	MD-88	9010
N910DL	MD-88	910
N911DE	MD-88	9011
N911DL	MD-88	911
N912DE	MD-88	9012
N912DL	MD-88	912
N913DE	MD-88	9013
N914DE	MD-88	9014
N914DL	MD-88	914
N913DL	MD-88	913

Regn	Aircraft Type	Fleet No
N935DL	MD-88	935
N936DL	MD-88	936
N937DL	MD-88	937
N938DL	MD-88	938
N939DL	MD-88	939
N940DL	MD-88	940
N941DL	MD-88	941
N942DL	MD-88	942
N943DL	MD-88	943
N944DL	MD-88	944
N945DL	MD-88	945
N946DL	MD-88	946

Left: *Just tucking up its undercarriage after take-off from Atlanta Worldport is MD-88 N977DL in March 1998.* Geoffrey P. Jones

Regn	Aircraft Type	Fleet No
N915DE	MD-88	9015
N915DL	MD-88	915
N916DE	MD-88	9016
N916DL	MD-88	916
N917DE	MD-88	9017
N917DL	MD-88	917
N918DE	MD-88	9018
N918DL	MD-88	918
N919DE	MD-88	9019
N919DL	MD-88	919
N920DE	MD-88	9020
N920DL	MD-88	920
N921DL	MD-88	921
N922DL	MD-88	922
N923DL	MD-88	923
N924DL	MD-88	924
N925DL	MD-88	925
N926DL	MD-88	926
N927DA	MD-88	927
N928DL	MD-88	928
N929DL	MD-88	929
N930DL	MD-88	930
N931DL	MD-88	931
N932DL	MD-88	932
N933DL	MD-88	933
N934DL	MD-88	934

Regn	Aircraft Type	Fleet No
N947DL	MD-88	947
N948DL	MD-88	948
N949DL	MD-88	949
N950DL	MD-88	950
N951DL	MD-88	951
N952DL	MD-88	952
N953DL	MD-88	953
N954DL	MD-88	954
N955DL	MD-88	955
N956DL	MD-88	956
N957DL	MD-88	957
N958DL	MD-88	958
N959DL	MD-88	959
N960DL	MD-88	960
N961DL	MD-88	961
N962DL	MD-88	962
N963DL	MD-88	963
N964DL	MD-88	964
N965DL	MD-88	965
N966DL	MD-88	966
N967DL	MD-88	967
N968DL	MD-88	968
N969DL	MD-88	969
N970DL	MD-88	970
N971DL	MD-88	971
N972DL	MD-88	972

Regn	Aircraft Type	Fleet No
N973DL	MD-88	973
N974DL	MD-88	974
N975DL	MD-88	975
N976DL	MD-88	976
N977DL	MD-88	977
N978DL	MD-88	978
N979DL	MD-88	979
N980DL	MD-88	980
N981DL	MD-88	981
N982DL	MD-88	982
N983DL	MD-88	983
N984DL	MD-88	984
N985DL	MD-88	985
N986DL	MD-88	986
N987DL	MD-88	987

Regn	Aircraft Type	Fleet No
N988DL	MD-88	988
N989DL	MD-88	989
N990DL	MD-88	990
N991DL	MD-88	991
N992DL	MD-88	992
N993DL	MD-88	993
N994DL	MD-88	994
N995DL	MD-88	995
N996DL	MD-88	996
N997DL	MD-88	997
N998DL	MD-88	998
N999DN	MD-88	999

McDonnell Douglas MD-88 fleet total — 120 aircraft

Left: *A McDonnell Douglas MD-88 surrounded by ramp equipment during a bank at Atlanta in April 1991, with other Delta MD-88s, DC-9s and Boeing 727s nosed in to Concourse 'C' beyond.* Geoffrey P. Jones

McDonnell Douglas (Boeing) MD-90

Regn	Aircraft Type	Fleet No
N901DA	MD-90-30	ex-N902DC
N902DA	MD-90-30	
N903DA	MD-90-30	
N904DA	MD-90-30	
N905DA	MD-90-30	
N906DA	MD-90-30	
N907DA	MD-90-30	
N908DA	MD-90-30	
N909DA	MD-90-30	
N910DN	MD-90-30	

Regn	Aircraft Type	Fleet No
N911DA	MD-90-30	
N912DN	MD-99-30	
N913DN	MD-90-30	
N914DN	MD-90-30	
N915DN	MD-90-30	
N916DN	MD-90-30	
N	MD-90-30	on order
N	MD-90-30	on order
N	MD-90-30	on order

A further 32 are on order